WINNING STRATEGIES

THE NEW RULES OF

RETIREMENT PLANNING

Good Selling

[signature]

MIKE McGLOTHLIN

ISBN-13: 978-1986698016
ISBN-10: 1986698017

The vast majority of this book was written on airplanes and in airports. That means that I spend a significant portion of my business life away from my wife, Alisa McGlothlin. This book represents the time and sacrifice she continues to make to support my career. Her ongoing support and love fuels me every day. I can never express the love, comfort and security that she provides me without even knowing she does it. Walking in and seeing her face when I return is still the best part of traveling.

I want to thank the entire staff at Ash Brokerage for helping our advisors help their clients retire more securely. In particular, Megen Gaylord, my retirement income sales coordinator, manages my social media posts, which is the genesis of this book. Tami Brigle has tirelessly read all my blogs multiple times and probably knows more about basketball and financial services than she cares to know. Jennifer Hendricks took ownership of the graphics and design for my books. But, our overall social media presence would not be possible without Ryan Benton, Troy Vian, Dean Oyer, Connor O'Shaughnessy and Toby Robles.

Finally, I want to thank all the financial professionals who are open minded to make the shifts that I write about in this book. Your clients undoubtedly enjoy a more secure retirement through innovative ideas and strategies that meet the growing risks associated with longevity and retirement. Our industry must continue to evolve in order to provide people with the most secure income in an ever-changing financial environment. I hope this book shows how our industry has changed – and where it needs to go in the future. I'm excited about how we can deliver our products and services to multiple generations to come.

Contents

Foreword

By Tim Ash, CEO, Ash Brokerage

If you embrace change, this book is for you. I've been in the financial services industry for nearly 33 years and never has there been such opportunity to embrace change, transform an industry and provide people with peace of mind in their financial lives. Tax reform, technology, politics, best interest standards, health care ... need I say more? All of it is noise. Clients are looking for trusted advisors to guide them.

Mike McGlothlin is the definition of a leader. He is a change agent who seeks solutions amidst the confusion advisors face. This book is filled with common sense wisdom and ways to chart a course for greater success and meaning in your financial services practice. It slices through the noise of the last two years by providing practical, insightful ideas around your business model, planning strategies and client experiences.

When you act on the ideas shared, I assure you great things will follow. I can say that with confidence as our firm is living proof. By adopting Mike's principles, Ash Brokerage is on track for 300 percent growth in less than five years. So, I urge and encourage you to heed his advice.

Thank you for your business and for making the financial services industry better.

Part I

External Factors of Change

My Fears of Change (of the Lack Thereof)

May 5, 2016

With the U.S. Department of Labor's rule still fresh in our minds, it's hard to think much beyond the changes our industry will face in the next 12 to 18 months. But, if we step back and look at the bigger picture, we have more important challenges ahead. We might be afraid of change, but I'm more worried about what will happen if we don't.

Lack of Advisors

In the United States today, we have only one financial professional for every 1,000 citizens. And, we have the largest generations of Americans leaving the workforce for retirement, relying on the assets they have saved for the rest of their lives. No way can a single professional provide the necessary advice to 1,000 people, especially with a low-interest environment, unstable global economy and the most complex tax code in history. We must develop a better system to recruit, invest in and train new professionals in our industry.

Commoditization of Technology

Technology can do great things for our industry, but it can also do some damage if we aren't careful. In his book, "End of Jobs," Taylor Pearson discusses how just a little over a decade ago, Loudcloud, an early cloud hosting service, hosted applications for $150,000 a month. Today, those same hosting services cost $1,500 a month.[1]

With today's appeal of the robo-advisor, I expect the same revenue compression over the next decade in our industry. Our current climate is to look for the least expensive way to provide a service instead of providing a service with the most value. Asset allocation can be found everywhere; however, managing the sequence of returns makes all the difference in whether a client runs out of money. We must redefine ourselves from asset managers to client-focused advisors – and customize it with scale.

Changes in Income

Pearson also points out that the American population faces a major shift in income generation – and he's not referencing the loss of earned income by voluntary retirement. Instead, more Americans will turn to entrepreneurial opportunities in the future. Because between 1948 and 2000, jobs grew 1.7 times faster than our population – since the turn of the century, however, our population has grown 2.4 times faster than jobs.

Without the retirement plans of "normal" employment, we must help our clients find vehicles to meet long-term savings demands and educate them on the impact of self-employment versus paid wages. Our clients started the mind shift, so our industry must adapt to keep up.

Moving Sooner than Later

It's been said many times, but it's worth repeating: We have to do a better job working on our business instead of in our business. It's time for us to make a fundamental shift, which requires thought and decisions on how we will capture market share in a largely homogeneous product set.

I challenge everyone to critically think about their business first thing, every day. In his book, "Triggers," Marshall Goldsmith discusses a 2011 study that followed 1,100 decisions of an Israeli parole board.[2] Seventy percent of the prisoners were granted parole when they appeared before the board in the morning, while only 10 percent received parole when they appeared in the afternoon. By human nature, we get fatigued and worn down by making decisions throughout the day, and we default to the status quo. My suspicion is that financial professionals end up with the status quo simply because we don't pay attention to our business until after we are too tired to think about our future.

We face a multitude of challenges in the next 12-18 months. All the while, the American population moves toward the need for more advice, more education, and a renewed industry full of fresh ideas and deeper client relationships – all energized by new technologies. We need to take time to think about how we exceed customer expectations – not by rates of return, but by experience.

Winning Strategy: Cost-conscious prospects looking for more advice create opportunities for the right business model. Have you spent enough time on your business so you can focus on its biggest assets – your clients?

[1]*"End of Jobs: Money, Meaning and Freedom Without 9-to-5,"* by Taylor Pearson: *http://www.amazon.com/End-Jobs-Meaning-9-5-ebook/dp/B010L8SYRG*
[2] *"Triggers: Creating Behavior that Lasts – Becoming The Person You Want To Be,"* by Marshall Goldsmith: *http://www.amazon.com/Triggers-Creating-Behavior-Lasts-Becoming-Person/dp/0804141231*

Chasing Product
May 12, 2016

Now that the U.S. Department of Labor's conflict of interest rule is out, we are beginning to hear rumblings of how advisors will react to the proposed changes. Most frequently, I'm hearing that advisors will remain focused on growing assets under management and distributing retirement income from assets using a systematic withdrawal plan. In this manner, they feel they won't interrupt their ongoing revenue stream.

This attitude is exactly why the DOL proposed the rule. If revenue (and any form of compensation) is your top priority, you are not acting in the best interest of your client. Instead, you need to identify the reasons why many consumers might be best served by fixed annuities, not just accumulating assets or variable annuities. For many years, fixed indexed annuities have provided similar, if not better, income riders for clients. Due to the stability of the accumulation value, carriers can better price the income benefit for clients.

When I hear annuity producers will change products because they can't earn a commission, I become concerned about where those producers might look for solutions. In recent years, the variable annuity industry has made their products more like commodities instead of their benefit-driven solutions of the past. By transitioning to fixed indexed annuities, I fear the industry will once again relent to irrational pricing that hurts all of us in the long run.

It appears that producers who are squirming for a viable solution didn't use the variable annuity chassis for upside potential, tax deferral or asset allocation strategies. Instead, they probably sold the product for its secondary guarantees on income. If the client needs income alone – and not the potential for cash accumulation, tax deferral and asset allocation – then they might be best served with alternative guaranteed income solutions like single-premium immediate annuities or deferred income annuities. With tax-favored distribution on nonqualified assets, the after-tax income level can be higher in these income solutions versus the typical variable annuity.

We have to change our focus. It's not about our old, antiquated business model anymore – it's about serving the client in ways we might not have looked at previously. The industry of tomorrow requires open-mindedness, unbiased discussions with clients and a continued willingness to learn new strategies to affect our clients' lives. Let's look at the fundamental shifts that the DOL wants our industry to comply with and make positive changes for our clients.

Winning Strategy: We're already seeing financial professionals scrambling for the next best solution to earn a commission. Let's start by dropping our biases toward solutions we are not familiar with and looking at new ways to solve client needs – even when we might not have done it before a fiduciary standard.

The Client Experience as an Innovation

May 26, 2016

With the new fiduciary rule in place, client experience will be the biggest differentiator of the future. Financial professionals can no longer run their businesses with the higher margin products and steady advisory fees we know today. We have to ask ourselves, "Is it easy to do business with me?"

Our customers take longer to plan for a vacation than they do for the next 30 years of their retirement. They require accuracy in their advice, but they also want speed and access in their relationship. In order to attract future generations of clients, we must fundamentally shift our business to a scalable model that features customization.

As financial professionals, our success requires that we not only reach but also communicate with a different generation. We are currently witnessing an epic transfer of about $12 trillion in wealth from the greatest generation to the baby boomers. And the boomers are expected to transfer some $30 trillion in assets to their heirs over the next 30-40 years.*

So, our industry must change as client needs change. Over the past 10-15 years, regulatory agencies and firms have stressed the impact of fees and assets under management. This made sense as the baby-boom generation completed its accumulation. Now, we must focus our attention on distributing the wealth our professional advice has helped to build. Those conversations are new to our clients and, in many cases, not our current expertise due to the bias of assets under management.

The fiduciary rules do not promote a doomsday event, but the financial professionals who will thrive through this change are those who fundamentally shift their thinking surrounding their business models and how they deliver products and services. While legislation forces change, the likely innovation comes in the form of better client experiences through technology and deeper relationships.

Improve your client experience for this generation and the next generation, and you will improve your financial planning practice.

Winning Strategy: Innovation comes in many forms. The fiduciary standard forces us to improve client experiences in order to succeed.

*Business Insider, "We're On The Verge Of The Greatest Transfer Of Wealth In The History Of The World," June 12, 2014: http://www.businessinsider.com/biggest-transfer-of-wealth-in-history-2014-6

Minutes to Memories …
What It Means for Our Industry

June 2, 2016

While I was in college, John Mellencamp enjoyed a lot of success, especially in the Midwest. During my senior year, I remember going to his sold-out concert at Indiana University's Memorial Stadium. Unfortunately, he didn't play one of my favorite songs, "Minutes to Memories" – one of his less popular tunes off the "Scarecrow" album from the mid '80s

The song is about a young man riding a bus overnight with an elderly man. Mellencamp eloquently shares the story that so many of us have been a part of – a wise person very senior in age gives a younger person the facts of life. The chorus repeats:

> *Days turn to minutes*
> *And minutes to memories*
> *Life sweeps away the dreams*
> *That we have planned*
> *You are young and you are the future*
> *So suck it up and tough it out*
> *And be the best you can*

I often listen to this song because our industry stands at a crossroads. Recent legislation has the potential to sweep away not only our dreams as financial professionals, but also the retirement dreams of many middle class Americans through the loss of quality financial advice. At the same time, we all have a chance to shape the future of the industry. No matter what the future holds, we need to tough it out and be the best financial professionals we can be.

As I have mentioned before, we must look at our business models, then adjust, adapt and grow as an industry. That means forcing carriers to be more client-friendly with ease of operations, access to information and better customer service for younger Americans.

It also means we have to evaluate our businesses and look to change the client experience. We must fight to show regulators we are capable of change that is both meaningful and lasting for our clients.

Stay tuned as the industry challenges regulations over the next couple of months. But, more importantly, stay focused on ways you can adapt your business to document the higher standards, act more efficiently and address the middle market concerns.

Winning Strategy: Keep your dreams – and your clients' dreams – alive. Let's figure out how to shape the future of our industry and make our businesses more efficient and effective.

Riding the Waves: How to Help Your Clients Cruise Through Retirement

June 9, 2016

Have you ever been on a cruise ship? The first day at sea can feel pretty strange, especially if it's a windy day and the sea is churning with waves. If you're not accustomed to walking on a ship, you might even find yourself holding on to the walls.

Though they may rock a little, cruise ships and other large vessels will continue cutting through the water with ease – they are built with a strong foundation and designed for balance.

Riding the Market Waves

Many Americans find their retirement vacillating on market returns, and early in 2016, the markets created choppy waters for those seeking steady income. So, how can you make sure your clients don't have to hang on to the walls through retirement?

Like a ship, they need a strong foundation and balance to cut through the waves. Without a doubt, a ship has to sway to some degree – just like a portfolio of well-balanced stocks and bonds. However, the variations in performance sometimes make things lean too far for a comfortable ride. No matter what happens, a strong foundation will bring their ship back to the middle.

Creating Strength and Balance

I'm not advocating everyone place their assets into instruments providing guaranteed income. Instead, I think you should consider a couple points when designing a portfolio for your clients.

1. You should take longevity off the table with a guaranteed, long-term income stream so your clients will not run out of money for essential living expenses

2. You should help provide inflation protection for future health care needs and overall growth

The next time you take on a retirement planning case, think about designing the portfolio like a ship. Guaranteed income will provide a strong foundation, and a selection of other assets can meet any needs that might arise and rock the ship.

Winning Strategy: A ship must be built to withstand all conditions – a retirement portfolio should be built the same way. Build a strong foundation and create balance so your clients can have smooth sailing through retirement.

What Happens on the Outside Doesn't Matter

June 16, 2016

Too often, we find ourselves caught up in the distractions around our work. Whether it's the interest rate environment, regulations or blanket recommendations from "experts" … Many times, we let the distractions dictate our decisions. No matter the client situation in front of us, too often, we revert back to our old planning techniques.

If we push the distractions aside, however, and focus on the needs of the people we serve, we're much more likely to succeed.

Hoosiers Hang Tough

At no surprise to those who know me, I was happy to see Indiana University win the 2016 men's basketball Big Ten regular season championship. If you don't follow IU basketball, you might be surprised to know the team was stumbling into the postseason a year prior.

Things were so bad, Coach Tom Crean was booed when he showed up to watch his son play at a high school basketball game. At the time, many Hoosier faithfuls were calling for his termination, and some even offered to pay for his buyout. The players also had several off-court incidents that were not indicative of IU basketball standards.

After coming back and winning the regular season championship in 2016, Coach Crean said the team didn't let the outside distractions impact how they prepared for games or used their strengths. He is quoted as saying:

> " ... *When you have faith in yourself and each other and what you're capable of, it doesn't matter what's said on the outside.*"

Why don't we do the same thing in business?

Focus on What Matters

No matter what happens in the months or years ahead, we have to keep the outside distractions on the outside and have faith in our financial planning process. The only thing that really matters is how our clients benefit from our recommendations. If we know that a purchase improves the client's situation (and we have faith in our products), we must stay focused on continuing to make the recommendation – even if regulations make it more difficult.

Winning Strategy: In all the changes to our industry, keep faithful in your financial planning process. Be open to change when it improves the client situation. And, keep distractions on the outside.

Intentional Influence: How to Choose Clients in a Post-DOL World

June 23, 2016

Each morning, I like to read a daily devotional or the Wall Street Journal – often both. Recently, I read two interesting things in one day: a passage about intentionality from Tony Dungy's "The One Year Uncommon Life

Daily Challenge," and an article about the meaning of the word fiduciary in the Journal's Wealth Adviser.

Coach Dungy, a TV sports show analyst and former Super-Bowl-winning coach, is a sought-after public speaker who could probably book any event he wants. However, he is intentional when selecting where he speaks and under what circumstances. Rather than accepting every offer, he evaluates where he can have the most positive influence.

What if we applied the same standards to our client relationships? It was very fitting I read the fiduciary article on the same day because I thought to myself how financial professionals will need to be more focused and intentional in their businesses going forward.

One of the collateral damages of the fiduciary rule is how we'll need to manage those clients who don't meet the criteria of taking the fiduciary risk while growing our businesses at the same time. I believe it starts with being intentional about the clients we choose and how we serve them going forward.

How many times have we been frustrated when clients don't provide the necessary financial statements at the discovery interview? Or when they fail to complete a medical exam for an insurance policy that will protect their families? What if we became more intentional about who we bring on as clients?

Consider setting some standards as you serve existing clients or bring on new ones:

- During the engagement process, evaluate your prospects' commitments to solving their financial needs – in a fiduciary world, we can no longer work with clients who are unwilling to participate in the financial planning process.
- Think about where and when you can have the most positive influence on your clients' financial plans, including asset management, retirement income planning and wealth transfer.

Winning Strategy: Think intentionally. Winners have a distinct set of parameters where they know they can succeed. Seek out those situations and take the necessary risks to grow your business.

Perspective, Gratitude and Pride for our Work

June 30, 2016

Perspective

While on a cruise, I got a painful, but much needed, bamboo massage. The therapist used hot oils to prepare my skin and muscles, then she proceeded to use a rolling pin-like bamboo instrument on me. It hurt, but it was the most beneficial and pain-relieving massage I'd ever experienced.

As I checked out of the spa, I signed the bill, which included a modest tip. I decided to add an additional tip for the therapist, and she handed it back to me, pointing out that a gratuity had already been added. I said I saw the gratuity but added some extra for the great massage.

She looked at me and questioned, "For me?" I nodded affirmatively, and she rigorously shook my hand. She went on to tell me that she had worked for the royal family in Saudi Arabia until joining the spa franchise, and where her family lives now, one dollar will buy five meals.

That's when perspective hit me squarely in the face.

Gratitude

I felt grateful to even have the option of getting a massage from this woman. And, I felt grateful to live in an economy as robust as ours, to be in the financial position to go on a great vacation with friends, have nice dinners and never worry about where my next meal was coming from.

As the day went on, I began to think about the value we bring to people as financial professionals. Much of our society isn't that different from the massage therapist – a small increase in money can be very meaningful. While it's not as extreme as her family's situation, millions of Americans face the challenge of living paycheck to paycheck.

More importantly, millions of Americans are NOT planning for a retirement that might include health care needs, inflation and longevity risks. How quickly will our country look like this woman's homeland, where too many people aren't able to enjoy the fruits of their labor?

Pride

I take pride in our staff and the work we do for our clients. And, I'm grateful our profession can have such a positive impact on so many people in the United States. However, there is much more work to be done, challenges to face and biases to eliminate.

Our industry – for all its faults – remains one of the most prestigious in the country. But regulators will continue to attack us due to the actions of an extremely small percentage of institutions and their employees – no different from any other industry. No matter what, we can control how we react and help Americans in the future.

Let's keep what we do in perspective and take pride in helping our neighbors make meaningful change in their financial lives.

Winning Strategy: Throughout life, you gain perspective from people you meet. We should take pride in helping people reach financial goals, no matter how large or small. Take time to reflect on your business, and be proud of the work you are doing.

Racing Toward Our New Future

July 7, 2016

In May, I attended the 100th running of the Indianapolis 500. It was an amazing event. With 350,000 fans packed inside the Indianapolis Motor Speedway, I think the race track became the 57th largest city in the United States that day. As I watched the race and walked around the speedway, I thought of all the history and tradition that makes up "The Greatest Spectacle in Racing."

Several aspects of the day stood out and made me think about how we conduct ourselves and run our business.

Respect

The Indy 500 always takes place on Memorial Day weekend, a holiday dedicated to honoring our veterans, especially those who gave their lives in service. In the race's opening ceremonies, "Taps" is played by a member of the military band. During the performance, you could hear a pin drop in the speedway – the atmosphere of respect was astounding.

The trumpet player captured everyone's attention and commanded their respect due to the meaning behind the ceremony. How do we gain that level of respect with our clients? Why can't we develop a rapport that makes them want to intently listen to every word (note) and reflect on what we say?

Courage

Due to the 100th running of the race, the speedway promoted the city of Indianapolis, which is only appropriate – it's a great place to live and grow up. The Indianapolis Children's Choir sang "God Bless America" and "America the Beautiful" before the race. A 10-year-old soloist performed flawlessly and made the hairs on my arm stand up. What courage for a 10-year old to stand up and sing in front of 350,000 people, plus millions more on television! She had to stretch herself to attain the confidence needed to perform on that stage.

Think about how many hours that little girl practiced for her three-minute performance. What did she do to become so focused that the distraction of thousands of people and cameras in her face didn't faze her a bit? Don't our clients deserve the same amount of focus and attention?

Strategy

Alexander Rossi won the Indianapolis 500 by driving across the finish line nearly on fumes. He strategized with his crew and made fewer pit stops by conserving fuel in the final laps. He painstakingly floored the gas and then coasted, holding the clutch in during the turns and short chutes. Then he ran out of fuel on his victory lap.

How much time do you spend working on your business instead of in your business? Rossi's crew knew how much mileage they would have throughout the race. Do you know how much revenue you are getting from each appointment, client or sales call? If not, you might find it more difficult to execute a new strategy as our business changes.

Winning Strategy: Think about how you can build trust and respect with your clients, have the courage to stretch and change, and create strategies that will propel your business forward.

Our Digital Value Dilemma

August 1, 2016

We're not in the technology industry, but it's clear technology is important to ALL industries, including financial services. As you evaluate your business model to meet new regulations, you should also consider how technology can make those changes more effective.

Recently, I read an article published by CISCO about digitization and the Global Center for Digital Business Transformation's 2015 study on digital disruption.* Digitalization, according to the article, refers to upgrading an office by creating a website or investing in cutting-edge technologies. By evaluating your own digitalization, you ultimately will be able to improve your client experience, a key differentiator that can set you apart from competitors. Advisors and financial planning firms that master this idea will stand a step above the rest.

The Cost of Waiting

The risk of NOT thinking digitally may prove costly. The Global Center's study predicts four of the top 10 industries will be replaced in the next three years due to "digital disruption" – when a technological advancement makes an industry nearly obsolete. For example, film cameras were replaced by digital cameras, and even digital cameras are now being replaced by smartphone cameras.

Failing to be up to speed with the digital world will result in being passed by those who have the technological advances. Our clients are bombarded by digital advertising and notifications, so we must remain at the forefront of their minds in order to capture market share. Only through a process of effective digitalization will our business be able to successfully reach clients and remain competitive.

Government regulation forces us to look at our business differently now, but technology can provide the tools we need to catapult our business to a higher level. As you evaluate changes to your practice, ask yourself:

- How can I become more technologically efficient as I market my services and products?

- More importantly, how can digitalization improve my client experience?

Both will help you increase your market share in the future.

Winning Strategy: Rethink your business model and client experience in order to improve. Don't allow new regulation to be the disruptor that solely shapes your business – use technology to make it more valuable to your clients and prospects.

Global Center for Digital Business Transformation, "Digital Vortex: How Digital Disruption Is Redefining Industries," June 2015: http://www.cisco.com/c/dam/en/us/solutions/collateral/industry-solutions/digital-vortex-report.pdf

How You Can Use the March Madness Mentality: Survive and Advance

August 8, 2016

If you know me, you know March Madness is one of my favorite times of the year. I love that the regular season, conference championships or even talent of the team doesn't matter once the tournament begins. Rather, what truly counts is how effectively the teams use the "survive and advance" strategy to play the next six games.

With all the recent changes in our industry due to the U.S. Department of Labor ruling, "survive and advance" certainly applies. Many industry experts continue to spew complaints, as the rulings' requirements are undoubtedly burdensome and difficult to administer. But instead of stagnating under the pressure, we need to adopt the "survive and advance" mentality – most importantly, we need to advance.

To advance your business, you should adopt this mentality in three areas:

1. **Fiduciary Standard** – As a financial professional, you must consider how to survive in a fiduciary role. Although many of you have already reached this standard with parts of your business, adapting your entire client base to that level may be difficult, timely and costly. You'll need to change your business

model and learn to become more efficient. However, these issues should be corrected and improved – with or without government requirements – to enhance your business. With the right mentality, these changes will not only help you survive, but also lead you to thrive.

2. **Technology** – Think of ways you can incorporate technology to improve your everyday practices and remain at the forefront of advances as they come. The true key to any change as a result of the DOL rulings will be how we advance with technology – as an industry and as financial professionals. Our banking industry competitors are able to move funds with the click of a cellphone camera. Yet, we still require timely paper signatures to move assets between carriers. Our current technological status and distribution methods will not attract millennials to invest in our business.

3. **Client Experience** – In a fiduciary world, it's ultimately the client experience, not the rule itself, that will determine who will be successful. If you can improve the client experience and attract new, high quality prospects, you will survive and advance. However, if you fail to step up your game, you will quickly fall behind.

Winning Strategy: Embrace the "survive and advance" mentality. Adapt to the specifics of the DOL ruling, but also think about advancing and thriving in your practice.

Why We Should Change Our Measurement of Success

August 15, 2016

When it comes to retirement planning, our industry's priorities need to change. If we continue to measure our success against the market, we'll always come up short of expectations.

Case in point: In March, the Wealth Adviser Daily Briefing from the

Wall Street Journal analyzed the benchmark performance for the mutual fund industry in 2015.* Some key takeaways:

- Not surprisingly, most stock pickers and active managers (66 percent) did not beat their benchmark index
- 84 percent of active large cap managers did not beat the Standard & Poor's 500 index over five years
- 82 percent did not beat the benchmark over 10 years

Obviously, there is a bias toward exchange-traded funds and index investing in today's planning. However, I argue there is another benchmark that is more important – the client's benchmark.

Clients rarely have a financial goal of exceeding the 10-year average of the S&P 500 performance. Instead, they usually have in mind a dollar amount where retirement seems achievable. We are noticing that dollar amount goal is shifting from a focus on the asset value to a focus on the amount of income that will make their retirement successful.

So, instead of publishing the performance of active managers against an external index, why don't we identify how many of their investors earned more than required in order to have a successful retirement? These investors should be held to the same fiduciary standard as the financial planners who are meeting with clients, working to ensure their goals are met. In a post-DOL world, we need to look at our entire industry differently and challenge our thinking as it relates to our clients' goals and objectives.

Going forward, we must align our goals with those of our clients in order to impact a meaningful change in our industry. The most successful financial planner will be someone capable of articulating how his or her financial planning process exceeded each individual client's benchmark return or income goal.

Winning Strategy: Instead of looking at external indices to validate our performance, let's focus on reaching our clients' goals first. Each client has a unique target they need to achieve in order to retire successfully – let's validate our success through their success.

*MarketWatch, "The S&P 500 beat 66% of stock pickers last year," March 10, 2016: https://www.marketwatch.com/story/the-sp-500-beat-66-of-stock-pickers-last-year-2016-03-10

Why We Can't Let Collaboration Die

August 18, 2016

Whenever someone enters my office, they are greeted by a picture of "The Last Shot." It captures the moment when Indiana University basketball player Keith Smart took the final shot of the game to help the Hoosiers win the 1987 National Championship. However, it's not just Smart I appreciate when I look at this picture. I also notice the other players, supporting him both on the court and on the sidelines. (EDITOR'S NOTE: *Mike is one of the people on the sidelines as a student manager.*)

Every time I look at this picture, I am reminded of the value of teamwork and collaboration. In a similar way, we must demonstrate a high level of cohesiveness to serve clients effectively. Our clients often trust us with their very last retirement dollar, and they deserve an extremely high level of professionalism in return.

Over the course of 30 years in this industry, I've observed a shift from holistic service to specialization. While the focus of retirement planning remains on accumulating assets, our clients need more than just asset management. Too little emphasis is placed on long-term care needs, guaranteed income floors and the transfer of wealth with the least amount of taxation.

Making Your Team Work

With the current DOL ruling defining new standards for our industry, are you capable of performing ALL the analysis necessary to serve your clients with excellence? My guess is that, individually, you aren't able meet that expectation. Therefore, you should use a more holistic, team-centered mindset to achieve these goals.

This type of collaborative plan can be executed with a variety of professionals:

- Life insurance agent
- Long-term care expert
- Attorney
- CPA

- And possibly others needed to serve the best interests of the client

When you use this approach, you must be certain everyone understands their roles as individuals and teammates. Regardless of who created the original plan for a client, everyone working on the case will also be held to the fiduciary standard, thus making it imperative for the team to work as a cohesive unit.

As you assemble your championship team, ask yourself a few questions:

- Are you willing to individually take on the fiduciary risk from others' recommendations?
- How can you ensure every team member is being transparent with the client about fees and disclosures?
- Is it time to rethink your business model as a sole practitioner and look to building a producer group that can address your clients' needs under one entity?

There's no doubt we must continue to collaborate for the benefit of our clients. The real question is how to do it effectively and efficiently for our business. Now is a great time to look at all your vendors as teammates and determine what gaps you need to fill. Just as a coach strategizes where to position certain players, you need to strategize with your carriers, vendors, services and technology.

When we surround ourselves with like-minded professionals, collaboration only benefits our clients. Think about how you will collaborate in a more regulated environment, and consider the consequences of working independently in a fiduciary setting while maintaining best interest standards. My fear is that collaboration will quickly fade as an unintended consequence of regulation and broker-dealer compliance. Teamwork is too important to lose as we transition into the next chapter of financial services.

Winning Strategy: Our strongest professional relationships might change as a result of regulation, but we can't sacrifice collaboration. You must be intentional about strengthening and maintaining your relationships, creating a team that will be effective for your clients and your business.

DOL Changes: What You Should Do First

August 29, 2016

*"Everyone has a will to win; few have a will to **prepare** to win."*
–Bob Knight, former Indiana Hoosiers basketball coach

With the new U.S. Department of Labor (DOL) rules coming into effect next year, many financial professionals are asking, "What do I *have* to do to comply?" I think the better question is, "What *should* I be doing to prepare?" Instead of focusing solely on what you must do, go a step further. Determine how you can enhance your business to not only comply, but also excel above the competition.

Critical Success Factors in Future Business Models:
- **Compensation regimes must remain as neutral as possible** – All revenue should be paid through an established grid so consumers are confident that conflicts are reduced.
- **Products with classes must become more uniform** – The DOL recognizes the time and effort devoted to some sales cycles for more complex and best interest sales. Differential compensation must be set by class, not individual product. Furthermore, all of us will need to work with smaller margins.
- **Conflicts of interest must be eliminated** – Metrics such as highly concentrated positions, high placement ratios of product classes and repetitive solutions must be addressed.
- **Distribution systems like career agencies add value in the oversight of producers** – It's essential to know your clients, agents and brokers in a fiduciary environment. Highly structured general agencies and offices of supervisory jurisdiction provide value and confidence when executed properly.
- **The fear of disclosure must be abandoned** – As an advisor, your recruitment process should educate your clients about disclosed information, including your commissions and

overall revenue into your firm. As a business owner, you shouldn't feel violated by the requirement to discuss your compensation regimes and business models. Your clients will appreciate learning why, how and what it takes to serve them with honesty and loyalty.

- **We have to keep our curiosity** – You must abandon your old biases in the former "suitable world" and remain open to different classes of assets and solutions to innovatively solve client needs.

While many uncertainties about the new rule remain, the DOL has indicated its willingness to provide guidance throughout the implementation period. However, the six items above will serve as a foundation for thought and action as the specifics are gradually clarified.

Winning Strategy: Preparing to win is more important than the desire to win. Use the DOL's implementation period to assess your business model and develop new strategies to deliver meaningful client solutions. Focus on improving methods of distributing products and services for future success.

How to Draft Your Team Like a Winning NFL Coach
September 1, 2016

In his daily devotional, "The One Year Uncommon Life Daily Challenge," former Indianapolis Colts coach Tony Dungy shares his strategy for selecting players in an NFL draft. As you may know, a team's draft pick can make or break a franchise because of the amount of time and money invested in each player.

During the draft process, Dungy evaluates the list of potential picks and writes DNDC ("Do Not Draft because of Character") next to the names of people with character flaws. This may seem harsh, but he understands the costly, long-term effects of having a player with poor character on his team.

Too often, teams seek short-term results while ignoring long-term problems. In order to avoid this pitfall, you should implement Dungy's stringent criteria when drafting your customer base. Similarly, your customers should use the same criteria when choosing you as their financial planning professional.

Drafting Your Best Team:

- Be someone of outstanding character who is worthy of being drafted by your clients
- Match your best practices with the right prospects – if your view of retirement planning does not align with your prospect's vision, you should have the fortitude to walk away from the potential business
- Don't be distracted by short-term results; remain focused on your clients' best interests over time – with increasing longevity, a retiree may be your client for at least 25-30 years, so it's critical to maintain a clear vision of their future
- Educate your clients on their need for a specific return, instead of only striving to beat the market index each year
- Constantly strive toward developing new alternatives and services – as millennials age and client demographics change, you must adapt to meet their needs, specifically through technology
- Remain flexible in an ever-changing world without compromising your long-term focus

Adjusting to the new fiduciary standards may seem difficult, but you can mitigate risks – for your clients and your business – by following Coach Dungy's simple rule: Do Not Draft because of Character.

Winning Strategy: Align the vision of the client, yourself and your staff in the retirement planning process. If you don't feel the client shares your long-term vision for their future, do not engage with them. Invest your time in better-suited clients and strategies to create your own winning team.

3 Steps to Get Out of Your Comfort Zone
September 8, 2016

As a child or a young professional, I never dreamed of being a writer. I simply didn't have the patience to stare at a blank page, waiting for the right words to come to mind. Over time, I've learned to rely on my expertise and passion for the subject to make it easier to begin the writing process. But to get to this point, I had to take the first step.

When I initially began writing blogs, they were inconsistent and infrequent. Gradually, as I changed my habits and made time to write blogs regularly, themes began to emerge and a clear niche evolved.

By practicing the habit of writing, I have developed a love for it. So much so, in fact, the editorial team probably pulls out their hair at times due to the mass quantity of content I throw at them. This passion for writing did not emerge naturally, however. I had to start with the basics and restructure my time to accommodate for this new hobby.

How I got out of my comfort zone:

1. **I developed the right mindset.** Habits are formed by a mindset, so you simply must change your mindset to change your habits. The fear of the new habit must be overcome with a clear understanding of the benefits of changing your behavior, and you must remind yourself of those benefits daily. Repetition creates consistency. Consistency breeds new habits.

2. **I made time.** Writing was an additional hobby that I wanted to adopt without replacing any of my existing work duties. When I examined my time, I realized that the long hours I spent on an airplane listening to music or simply staring at the seat in front of me could be used more productively. Establishing a new habit to occupy previously "wasted time" seemed like an effective strategy.

3. **I executed.** On every flight segment, I challenged myself to write one blog. I would use the quiet time on the plane to concentrate

my thoughts and ideas into coherent written words. Over time, I developed consistency, and the task of writing became far less daunting. I also expanded my knowledge of content marketing to refine my skills, and passion and expertise soon emerged.

When the Ash Brokerage creative staff approached me about compiling the blogs into books, it took me by surprise. I never imagined myself as a published author. It took some time to get used to the idea, but, in the end, I'm glad decided to step outside of my comfort zone. By taking the first step and forming a new habit, I now have two books on Amazon that hopefully give advisors like you motivation, new ideas and helpful strategies to better serve your clients.

Winning Strategy: Get out of your comfort zone and try something new. You may be surprised by how much you enjoy the experience of pushing your limits and challenging your capabilities. New habits can improve your personal and business life immensely. Take the first steps: develop the right mindset, set aside time and execute.

The Real Problem with Retirement Planning
September 22, 2016

Some people claim the U.S. Department of Labor (DOL) conflict of interest rule is ruining the retirement industry. But, have you ever thought that maybe the industry is ruining retirement?

According to a 2015 article from U.S. News and World Report, Americans aren't saving enough.* While the DOL implementation and other market shifts certainly affect retirement trends, at the end of the day, Americans simply aren't prepared for retirement. Imagine having $212,000 set aside for retirement with no further chance to earn income. And, it must last you the rest of your life.

In reality, the retirement industry may have created this problem. For the past two decades, I've been told to focus on building a renewable income stream for myself. But, in order to do that in a productive business model, most planners must move up market and set minimum asset levels to engage new clients. The problem is millions of Americans have failed to work with financial professionals early in their careers to develop well-allocated, systematic savings plans. Now, they are suffering the consequences.

The DOL is attempting to level the playing field, but collateral effects include the commoditization of our business. How can you make your business stand out from the rest and make a difference in your clients' lives while the industry continues to make the same mistakes?

Strategies for Improvement:

- Evaluate your business model and target markets in light of the DOL rulings to ensure excellence in products and services
- Focus on serving the middle class through education and strategy, as this population is ill-prepared for retirement, both financially and emotionally
- Initiate income planning conversations with Americans of all ages whenever the opportunity arises
- Utilize effective tools that provide relief for past years of ignoring the problem

Winning Strategy: Seize the opportunity to support the underserved middle class in America. Moreover, discover market niches that boost productivity for you and your business as you navigate the post-DOL world.

U.S. News & World Report, "Almost Half of Americans Aren't Saving Nearly Enough," March 30, 2015: https://www.usnews.com/news/articles/2015/03/30/almost-half-of-americans-arent-saving-nearly-enough

How You Can Overcome Constraints Like Super Mario

September 29, 2016

A constraint is often seen as a limitation. However, true innovators see a constraint as an opportunity for improvement and creativity. It's an opportunity to not only overcome obstacles, but also to improve upon the processes and solutions we use when problems arise.

Constraints come in many forms. In the financial services industry, our constraints include:

- Time
- Resources
- Technology
- Regulations
- Market conditions, especially when experiencing volatility or low yields

Regardless of your perceived limitations, you can produce creative solutions for your clients and the industry.

Constraints Lead to Creation

Mario is an iconic video game character, but the story of his creation isn't as well-known. Have you ever wondered why Mario wears his hat, gloves, overalls and huge mustache? All of those features helped his developers overcome constraints.

They didn't have enough pixels to make Mario's hair flop or bounce as he moved through the game, so they gave him a hat. They also didn't have enough time or resources to design a mouth, so they gave him a bushy mustache. Finally, limited ability prevented them from creating a shirt, buttons or belt buckle, so – you guessed it – they gave Mario overalls.

As you can see, great successes can emerge from great constraints. As increasing regulations, changing interest rates or volatile markets seem to place undue constraints on your business, use them as an opportunity to separate yourself from the competition, be creative and provide a unique solution for your clients.

Winning Strategy: Use constraints as an opportunity to differentiate yourself in the marketplace, make unique solutions and improve processes.

If You Knew Then What You Know Now

October 6, 2016

You've probably heard the phrase, "Hindsight is 20/20" or, "Looking in the past is the clearest way to see the future." While these phrases are often true, people don't always learn from their mistakes – especially when it comes to investment decisions.

In summer 2016, our market experienced record-low Treasury yields. During that time, many clients and advisors failed to review historical trends and move assets into alternative investments.

Looking back over the past 10 years, numerous financial and non-financial events rocked the market. Did you and your clients invest funds strategically in response to these events, or did you miss a good opportunity?

- The mortgage crisis of 2007 caused many investors to run from securities. But those who kept their ground are now reaping the rewards after the market reached record highs in summer 2016.

- In 2009, the swine flu appeared to be a catastrophic pandemic, sending many people into a financial frenzy. Yet, for those who remained invested during that time, the yield was nearly 5 percent.

- When the United States' credit rating was downgraded in 2011, many predicted a yield increase to reflect the rising risk associated with the downgrade. Surprisingly, the yield fell substantially.

While you should be optimistic about yields increasing over the next three to five years, you must still get your clients focused on how to generate income in retirement. You can't allow the past to dictate your clients' future. Clients are often focused on reasons not to save or invest, so it's crucial to educate them on the proper products and asset allocation to maximize their portfolio.

Winning Strategy: While clients often allow past economic conditions to dictate their current financial decisions, take the opportunity to educate them about promising investment opportunities and optimize their funds to achieve their retirement goals.

Fundamental Truths of Chasing Yield and Liquidity

October 13, 2016

I have long discussed the need to position your products and services on value propositions rather than rates. However, I want to talk about the advantages of selling in today's low-rate environment and placing the client in a better position using rate as an example. In the long run, the value you bring to your clients by talking about current fundamentals will bring more people back to your office.

As I look at today's rates (Sept. 6, 2016), the current 30-year Treasury Yield is 2.24 percent. Several insurance carriers are offering five-year, multiyear guaranteed annuities with similar rates. In the Wall Street Journal, I constantly read about advisors placing their clients in dividend-paying stocks to create better yields in the portfolio. So, in order to obtain higher yields, the client either must take equity risk in the portfolio or expose the bond portion of the portfolio to extreme price depreciation in the event of a rising interest rate market. Neither sounds fundamentally strong for the long haul.

Too many advisors fail to show an alternative because of their own biases against annuities or bad past experiences. I believe we are in the best-ever market conditions to sell our products. Even with fixed annuity yields between 2.25 percent and 3.34 percent (assuming an FIA hits a 4.5 percent cap 75 percent of the time), our taxable equivalent yield is, at a minimum, 3.84 percent – well above the current investment-grade corporate bond yields. The nominal return is just as high as the current 30-year Treasury rate, with no risk to principal in an increasing interest rate environment.

So, while your competition searches for the next best thing that their clients want to hear or chase, talk to your prospects and clients about two fundamentals: safety and liquidity. Ask yourself:

- Why wouldn't your client want to take a 30-year yield with one-sixth of the maturity?
- Why wouldn't the client want to have a more liquid portfolio for the same yield with additional flexibility for emergencies

and medical issues?

- What prevents you from showing this option? Likely, it's your mindset against a lower interest rate than six months ago.

Winning Strategy: Don't focus on where the economy or interest rates were six months ago and compare them to today. Look at the relative economic conditions and talk to your clients about fundamentals. They will appreciate the simple, straight-forward approach to their retirement success.

Happy Birthday, Mediocrity!

October 20, 2016

At the end of August 2016, the Vanguard Group's First Index Investment Trust turned 40. While many people laughed at John Bogle as he rolled out low-cost investing designed to match the index instead of beating it, the fact is that the Standard & Poor's 500 index now stands at $252 billion in assets.

Client sentiment has changed since the launch of indexing. Between the concept and the perception, our world evolved to embrace mediocre investment performance subsidized by low-cost management.

Over the past four decades, the philosophy of matching the index instead of outpacing it grabbed the attention of many clients. While most managers do not beat the index, it's problematic that too many indices are measured against the S&P 500. Many funds are not meant to beat the benchmark because the manager might reduce an exposure to undue risk, for example.

Of course, the advantage of indexing is to do so in a low-cost manner. According to the Wall Street Journal, Vanguard has reduced investment fees by as much as 90 percent.* In the end, whether it is cost or performance, indexing seems to have won out against the active manager. Even the U.S. Department of Labor mentions indexing as a viable alternative for retirement investors.

*So, if fees are near minimum and matching the index
is a desired investment return, how can a financial professional
add value to his/her financial planning practice?*

The answer lies in getting clients to consider other things besides return. We need to change our approach ...

- As our population ages, we must show inflation-adjusted, after-tax income (not returns) to our clients
- Conversations about longevity will become more important than conversations about asset allocation
- For more Americans, affording the same essentials 20 years into retirement will be more of a concern than the amount of equities they have in their portfolio
- It will be more valuable to know our clients' portfolios won't be devastated if a health care event happens, compared to knowing how much they earned in one year
- Talking about how we can protect our clients' legacies for the next generation will be more powerful than talking about how we reduce investment risk

Being able to execute on those value propositions will be more important in the future. Just as Vanguard changed the conversation to cost and return, we should change the conversation to protection, income and longevity to add value in the long run.

Winning Strategy: Look at how Vanguard has changed the dynamic of investing since 1976. Indexing drove the investing population to high cost and little value. Drive your clients to valuable services like reducing longevity risks, creating legacy values for the next generation and protecting their wealth.

*The Wall Street Journal, "Wealth Adviser Daily Briefing: Index Funds turn 40, a 'How-to' for Foreign Home Buyers," Sept. 1, 2016: http://blogs.wsj.com/ moneybeat/2016/09/01/wealth-adviser-daily-briefing-index-funds-turn-40-a-how-to-for-foreign-home-buyers/

Jump-Starting Slumping Sales

October 27, 2016

I have always been told the sales business is like a teenager's first car – if you turn the car off to get gas, you aren't 100 percent sure it will start again. It inevitably does, but you really have to work at it.

The summer lull is over and many advisors tell me they don't have a reason to contact their clients. The stock market continues to be bullish and clients aren't complaining. Low interest rates don't seem attractive enough to reach out to clients. There is a lot of complacency in our industry.

Let me give you three reasons to contact your clients right now:

1. **Take the option to lock in some gains.** The stock market has reached several all-time highs in recent months. There are many signs that the market growth has slowed, or it may be ready to turn to a bear market. Certain indicators, such as high price-earnings ratios and dividend yields, resemble those of the pre-financial crisis. Talk to your clients about sweeping gains out of their individual retirement accounts using a tax-free direct transfer to lock in the gains from the account. You can protect your clients from a potential bear market and still keep them linked (subject to caps) to equity indices or asset allocation strategies.

2. **Reduce the risks of longevity in the portfolio.** The No. 1 fear of Americans remains living past their assets and not having enough income. You can reposition your client's portfolio, maybe making the portfolio more efficient, by implementing a deferred income annuity strategy. This will help take some longevity risk off the portfolio by making sure your client has income for the rest of their life, irrespective of their asset values.

3. **Consider positioning bond portfolios against rising interest rates.** Earlier this year, the 10-year Treasury reached an all-time low. While no one can predict when rates will rise, the

Federal Reserve has signaled a potential increase in interest rate policy. This will eventually have a ripple effect on bond prices. Take the time to sit down with clients and talk about that risk. Annuities as short as a five-year duration provide higher yields than 30-year Treasurys as of today (Sept. 9, 2016). Now is a perfect time to diversify the interest rate risk and protect bond portfolio values.

Those are just a couple of reasons you should call clients now. If they don't start your sales engine, you might have to keep trying to start that old car. Too often, we get lazy as an industry and think that because our clients aren't calling us they don't want to hear from us. I challenge you to think differently. I suspect our clients want to hear from us. In fact, they probably think that's why they are paying us – to reach out and lead them through the complexities of retirement income planning.

Winning Strategy: Don't wait for clients to reach out with a difficult situation. Take the initiative to reach out to your clients now and give them options to protect their retirement income savings.

Seeking Income Replacement with Low Interest Rates

November 3, 2016

Near the end of August, my daily Google search brought something to my attention. An article, "Advisers seek income replacement as interest rates tumble," addressed how financial planners are looking at changing the conversation with their clients to increase the return and yield in their portfolios.* There were some interesting statements made in the article that I think need to be discussed.

1. The firm highlighted in the story manages to the asset return minus inflation. They are targeting a long-term return of 3.5 percent to 4.0 percent, which is very reasonable. However, their model portfolio to achieve those returns consists of 25-30 percent fixed income and 70-75 percent equities. Even for

a 60-year-old with a long life expectancy, that concentration in equities presents some risk that many may not be willing to take. And, even with conservative returns, longevity risk has not been addressed – the client can still run out of money. With a 70 percent allocation into equities, sequence of return risk remains high, even though the equity portion is well diversified.

2. The firm states that if the client can't settle for an annual 3 percent return, it recommends a 90 percent equity allocation. Obviously, the client's risk tolerance must support this. However, chasing return tends to make portfolios more aggressive, increase turnover costs and increase tax exposure to nonqualified portfolios. Planners need to be careful about allocation strategies that tend to drift to more aggressive. I like to remind clients they never know how much risk to take until they have taken too much. Additionally, the firm looks to add illiquid vehicles to boost yield. Again, as we look toward retirement, the need for liquidity and uncertainties mount. The need for liquidity might increase as we move from our working years to our non-income-producing years.

3. The article failed to address other risks to the portfolio besides market risk. Planners tend to address market and return risk through allocation strategies. However, there are so many other risks for a near retiree or retiree. Successful plans mitigate longevity risk and make the portfolio more efficient, provide access to affordable health care options, provide a strategy to maximize Social Security, address the potential effects of a chronic or unexpected illness, mitigate long-term care expenses associated with a nursing home or in-home health care expenses and much more.

We have slipped into a world of asset managers and asset gathers. Being fiduciaries means looking out for our clients' best interests – that includes not only asset growth, but also asset protection. By protecting assets, we can eliminate pressure on the remaining assets that would have required a higher return. By reducing longevity risk, we may be able to lower the required return and adjust equity allocations to normalized allocation percentages for retirees.

Winning Strategy: Address the entire financial plan, not just the assets under management. Too many firms concentrate on asset growth and using asset growth to replace income. That type of portfolio is tax and cost inefficient. We need to look at alternatives that can protect the portfolio while mitigating the other risks associated with retirement income planning. It's not as simple as changing an allocation.

FinancialPlanning, "Advisers seek income replacement as interest rates tumble," Aug. 29, 2016: http://www.financial-planning.com/news/advisers-seek-income-replacement-as-interest-rates-tumble

Get Creative on Your Playground

November 10, 2016

Recently, I've been reading a book, "A Beautiful Constraint: How to Transform Your Limitations into Advantages, and Why it's Everyone's Business," by Adam Morgan and Mark Barden. I would highly recommend it to any financial professional thinking about how to implement changes to their practice. And, a couple of weeks ago, I witnessed an analogy the authors use to discuss creativity.

I was walking home to meet a repairman when I noticed students at a nearby school were out to recess. As I waited for the repairman to show up, I watched the children play on the playground. They ran freely around the designated area, which was enclosed by a chain-linked fence. They pushed the boundaries of the recess zone – some were even climbing up the fence and had to be told to get down. They made up their own games with their friends, played hide-and-seek and generally let their minds run free and enjoyed themselves.

In contrast, I recently witnessed a class of children attending a day game for Fort Wayne's single-A baseball team, the TinCaps. As I walked to lunch that day, the kids were in an open area, yet all of them were milling around within 10 feet of their teachers. There was no hide-and-seek, no one running to climb a nearby wall, and no one making up their own games. Instead, with all this wide-open space, they were listening carefully to their instructor and waiting for the next order. The lack of constraint didn't foster creativity.

It's the same with business constraints – they can set up and provide a launching pad for creativity. Without constraints, we tend to follow orders or continue to do what we think is successful – probably because it's the way it worked previously. Instead, we need to push our limits and look for new ways to attack our clients' problems.

It's constraints like the U.S. Department of Labor (DOL) fiduciary rule that force us to look at our clients' needs differently … more creatively. This is a time to rethink how you provide guaranteed income to your clients and secure their financial future. Take the opportunity of the regulatory constraint to grow your financial planning practice through creative ideas and strategies, solving problems with open mindedness toward solutions that are new to you, and introduce your clients to a more holistic experience in a post-DOL world.

Winning Strategy: A constraint can challenge you to look at your financial planning practice differently. Use the current regulatory constraints to look at expanding your offerings and make your business more holistic. You will likely capture more business from existing clients.

Which Risk Do You Want?

November 17, 2016

Since the U.S. Department of Labor (DOL) rule was announced in April 2016, there have been so many interpretations of the rule and its effects on individual financial planning firms. As I read the rule in April, one of my biggest concerns was that advisors would shift their product mix to the path of least resistance instead of really digging into what might work for the client.

Unfortunately, I see and hear a lot of "I'm not going to sell annuities in the future." Even worse, I continue to hear broker-dealers limiting product menus to make compliance easier.

Over the last several years, the stock market has been on one of the longest bull runs in history. In July and August 2016, I watched the stock market hitting all-time highs. But, at the same time, I saw inactivity at the advisor and client levels. The annuity industry reports sales slowing during the summer months across most carriers. Our business has slowed and our sales teams report that clients don't want to meet with their financial advisors. In turn, advisors have begun to turn their clients' accounts into fee-based accounts after charging an upfront commission. In many cases, they feel the change is mandated by their firm. Many are not taking the opportunity to advise clients – instead, they are just focusing on the administrative change in compensation.

Unfortunately, through all the DOL issues, we have failed to focus on what is most important: protecting our clients' retirement income savings and income potential. With markets growing to all-time highs and volatility low, it seems like a perfect time to remain invested. However, when you look at extended periods of low volatility heading into the fall months, you see an increased period of volatility after Labor Day. Our clients, especially those within five to 10 years of retirement, have too much to lose in the next market downturn.

So, my question is simple:

Do you want to be protected from regulatory risk by not selling annuities under a Best Interest Contract? Or, are you exposing yourself to litigation risk by not reaching out to clients and locking in gains with a significant risk of account value loss?

Too often, we get caught up in media and peer conversations about the regulatory environment changes. Make no mistake, the changes coming in April 2017 are significant. But, it's no reason to abandon our clients and stay within our comfort zone of asset management. Instead, it's a time to reflect on the entire value proposition you bring to the table for your clients. More importantly, it's time to act upon protecting their retirement savings before the next market correction.

Winning Strategy: Take a look at your clients who are within five to 10 years of retirement. Call them for a meeting to assess their current risk tolerance and desire to take some of the investment risks off the table.

A Call for More Financial Professionals

November 24, 2016

With the U.S. Department of Labor conflict of interest and fiduciary rule looming, many people predict a loss of sales and financial professionals. I've talked extensively about the opportunity to expand one's financial practice, but I fear the new rule will create a barrier to entry for many individuals – young and old – thinking about a financial services career.

A recent study by The American College found a large segment of the population scored poorly on a financial literacy test, indicating a tremendous need for retirement education, which can best be served one-on-one and face-to-face, not through a digital interface.

Below are some key findings from the RICP Retirement Literacy Survey:*

- Only 19 percent passed the retirement income quiz (scoring 60 percent or better). Not one person in more than 1,000 respondents received an A (90 percent or better). And, only 1 percent of the respondents scored a B (between 80-90 percent).

- Only 39 percent of respondents knew that when interest rates rise, bond prices drop. With today's low interest rate environment and people reaching for longer durations, the risks associated with bond ownership has never been higher. The majority of Americans don't understand the direct correlation and the effects of changes in interest rates.

- More than half the respondents underestimated the life expectancy of a 65-year-old male. Too often, robo-advisors guide a client through some assumptions, but the action is left to the person selecting the input. This survey result suggests half of Americans underestimate how long they will need their assets to last.

- Only 31 percent of people responding to the survey knew that 4 percent can be safely withdrawn from an account during retirement (the 4 percent rule). Even with increased media attention to retirement income and focus on decumulation strategies on digital platforms, most people do not understand how much they can withdraw from their savings.

All of the above (and similar statistics from the survey) should alarm you about the readiness of most Americans as they move toward retirement. When we are unprepared, we have to seek out professional assistance. That assistance is not going to come from a robo-advisor or digital platform. Clients need, and deserve, to feel comfortable and have their questions answered. More importantly, they should have a relationship that challenges them to think about potential risks like longevity, health care, interest rates, rate of return targets and income strategies.

It's unlikely that a computer program will have the expertise to direct a client through the complexities of retirement planning and be there to make them feel comfortable when the plan may bend off course.

Winning Strategy: Think about providing more education to your clients and prospects. Surveys point to a need for more education. More importantly, there is a need for more financial professionals to help execute meaningful financial plans. Help someone into our industry and be a mentor to them.

The American College, "6 Disturbing Findings from America's Failed Retirement Quiz," Aug. 10, 2016: http://knowledge.theamericancollege.edu/blog/6-disturbing-findings-from-americas-failed-retirement-quiz

3 Ways to Get More from Your Brain

December 1, 2016

Like many professionals, I try to incorporate meditation into my daily routine. With meetings for seven to eight hours of the day and many nights taken up by client dinners, I find it difficult to be present while at home or to simply rest my mind. It's hard to start a new habit, especially when you don't feel results immediately. However, I know in the long run meditation will make me healthier and help me make better decisions for my sales division.

One of the reasons I started to look into meditation was the advice from my business coach. But, I found a lot of other information and reasons why I needed to "rest my brain" occasionally.

Did you know the brain completes 1,000,000,000,000,000,000 calculations per second? That's right – it's a one with 16 zeros after it. I had to look up the proper name for the number – it's quintillion. I just knew it was a big number.

Think about the brain's capacity and its limitations. It takes the brain approximately 21 minutes to refocus on a complex task after being interrupted. But, at the same time, it can conduct 1 quintillion calculations per second. So, how do you manage this important part of the human body and maximize its use for clients?

1. **Focus** – Given our busy schedules (and our clients), it's imperative we keep the mind on task. I recommend time-blocking for important activities like calling clients, client appointments and managing your business. Focusing on tasks allows you to leverage the power of your brain and its massive computing ability.

2. **Rest** – It's important to rest your brain and keep it fresh. After all, it's really working overtime doing all those calculations. Take time to enjoy the outdoors; sit and listen to "nothing" – chirping, whispering, glistening or whatever you hear. Enjoy the moment. Allow the brain to relax and take in the environment. By having a relaxed brain, you are in a better position to make great decisions about your business and with your clients.

3. **Challenge** – Lately, I've been talking a lot about constraints. Challenge your brain to think outside the normal flow of business. Ask yourself, "Is there a better solution for my client that provides a better outcome than how I am doing it now?" Your clients will appreciate the ideas that your brain delivers. After all, one idea out of a quintillion isn't all that hard, right?

Winning Strategy: Allow your brain to rest periodically. And, when it's time to focus, make sure you are uninterrupted. The level of productivity you enjoy will surprise you. Practice exercising your brain just like the rest of your body.

Interest Starts Change

December 8, 2016

I recently spent a couple of beautiful days in Washington, D.C. Although many people were on fall break visiting our nation's capital, I was not. My days were spent preparing for, and talking to, members of the U.S. Department of Labor. I found the experience intriguing, interesting and awkward – all rolled into one. But, significant change requires all those factors.

As financial professionals, we must always be intrigued by our fiduciary responsibilities to our clients, even if we believe we are already providing that level of care. No matter your specialty or the focus of your financial services practice, you have to think about all the possible ways of improving a client's position. This is exactly why the department allowed us to come in and discuss our concerns. They were as intrigued as we were about the opportunity to improve the distribution of financial advice. I believe that level of intrigue is good for our industry.

In order to improve, you must have an interest in change – far more than mere intrigue. We must have a sincere interest in changing how the industry provides better options and service to our clients. The department displayed a genuine interest in improving and understanding the market for annuities and life insurance. With a genuine interest in improving, we typically move to the awkward stage – where you feel you need to change your behavior.

The new fiduciary rule requires significant changes of behaviors at every level of our industry, perhaps even a change in behavior from the department, as well. Regardless, when you change the way you do things, there is a feeling of awkwardness. But, there is always a path to change through understanding and repetition. If you are intrigued and interested in getting better, you will do the uncomfortable things until they become comfortable. In the end, you will have to go through all the stages in order to improve.

Winning Strategy: Find something that intrigues you about your business. Get interested in why the process works the way it does. Get uncomfortable with a new process or product.

Adversity: A Different Perspective

December 15, 2016

Challenges can come in many forms, sneaking in slowly but then spiraling out of control. How many times have you described a sales slump just like that? I've certainly had my share of slumps during my nearly three-decade career, and I think it's important to look inside the problem to keep the adversity in perspective.

First, we have to look at the root cause of any adversity. This may seem easy, but almost always the obvious cause is not the real cause. You have to look deeper than just looking at the obvious. Key performance indicators (KPIs) are a great place to start, but even KPIs might not show the heart of the problem. You have to ask yourself, "Why is this KPI looking like this? What might I unknowingly be doing that creates these results?"

As I frequently suggest, behavior change is not only difficult but also at times painfully slow. Recognizing the problem early is critical to lessening the effects of poor performance. But stopping the patterns of behavior that are causing the problem is only the first part.

Once you have determined the cause of adversity, you have to keep that challenge in perspective. Recently, I measured our performance against different industry benchmarks in several distribution channels. Even though our activity and effectiveness were not up to our normal KPIs, I found our sales numbers were much better than industry averages. Now, that doesn't mean we don't need to change, but the numbers do help me keep our current activity in perspective. And, it helps me provide information to my sales team that keeps them energized. When our competition is suffering, that is the time to capture market share, not to say, "Everyone is affected, so we are just fine." We still have to focus on the root cause of adversity to deal with it.

At the end of the day, adversity provides an opportunity for improvement. But it's important not to correct the same problem time after time. Each cycle of adversity generally creates unintended and unexpected consequences for our actions. Look at adversity as a chance to improve. When you do, a challenge doesn't seem as bad and can even be a sign of healthy growing pains.

Winning Strategy: Don't hang your head during times of adversity. Look at adversity as a learning tool. Identify the root cause and work on correcting it, but keep the adversity in perspective to your overall business. Make sure you don't over correct, but rather use adversity as an opportunity to grow through change.

Connecting to Our Clients

December 22, 2016

Living in Fort Wayne means I can usually find very few direct flights. On a recent connection at a national "hub" airport, my plane was running a few minutes late. So I had a chance to sit down, eat my dinner of M&Ms I'd bought at a kiosk, and relax for about 20 minutes.

I chose a bench facing the middle of the concourse and began watching people pass me one-by-one. Some were running to their next connection; others dragging their children through the concourse.

A few were simply strolling through the airport, while most were walking briskly. One poor soul was just leaning against the handrail on the moving sidewalk after an exhausting day of travel.

Where were they all going?

Why were they going there?

What could they all be doing that had to be done at that particular location?

Why was it so important?

For a tired annuity wholesaler, these were monumental questions. But I think these are the same questions our clients deserve. The only difference is to add "in retirement" to the end of the question.

Where are you going in retirement?

Why are you going there in retirement?

What has to be done at that particular location in retirement?

Why is it so important in retirement?

If we ask those questions, I bet we find out a lot about the lifestyles our clients want in their retirement. Where? Why? What would they be doing? Having those issues out on the table can guide us to solutions that will be most meaningful to those we serve.

By the way, stop and say hello the next time you see a middle-aged man in a suit and tie sitting in a concourse eating M&Ms.

Winning Strategy: Ask the right questions and get the correct answers to your clients' most heartfelt goals for a successful retirement.

Getting Better Every Day

December 29, 2016

I'm not sure about you, but the Garmin advertising campaign excites me every time I see it. It works around the idea of beating yesterday's performance. As I train for a half-marathon, I'm constantly reminding myself that it's about getting better after several years away from running. Regardless of where your financial services practice is today, you should adopt the same philosophy when it comes to preparing for the U.S. Department of Labor (DOL) fiduciary and conflict of interest rule.

With more than 1,000 pages of text, the new rule can be overwhelming. At times, I find myself wondering how our firm will be able to adapt to all our interpretations of the rule. But, growth and change happens gradually. I say, "by baby steps" on many occasions. You have to beat the previous day.

So, what can you do today in order to move the needle forward, if ever so slightly, from yesterday?

First, I encourage you to look at your books of business and review your exposure to the rule. You should be working with your marketing organization or broker-dealer to see how their interpretation of the rule will impact your client files. Segmenting the clients with qualified accounts would be a great start.

Next, I think it is important to look at where you want your practice to be in the next three to five years. There are two main questions I think you have to consider when preparing for the DOL rule: Are you going to move up market? Or, are you going to become more efficient in your current market?

Both are viable options, but how you want your practice to look in the future should dictate how you approach your clients today. If you are moving up market, you will need to begin addressing protection and longevity needs. If other producers are vacating your market, you need to think about how you can capture market share. Regardless, you need to think about how you plan to grow your existing business.

Neither one of those strategies happens overnight. You must begin to take the baby steps necessary to gain control of your future business. Think about what you have to do today that will make your life easier after the rule takes effect in April 2017. You will be glad you prepared.

Winning Strategy: Adapting to the new fiduciary standards takes time. You can't jump off the couch and run a marathon. You need to improve little by little. The same goes for preparing for the new rules. Think about how you can improve today in a way that will positively impact your practice after April 2017.

Industry Changes

January 5, 2016

If you ask most people what the biggest change the financial services industry is facing, they will likely say regulation. The U.S. Department of Labor's fiduciary standard and conflicts of interest rule has certainly captivated everyone's attention for more than a year. Regardless of implementation date, firms across America are already changing how they conduct business. But, regulation is only a small percentage of the changes that likely will force us to change our practices – and for the better.

Several trends will impact the expectations of our clients in the future as they plan for retirement. Each creates a certain amount of risk, but three in particular will force us to have a different kind of conversation with our clients than we've had in the past.

Growth of Defined Contribution Plans

For decades, the number of participants in defined contribution plans grew, while participation in defined benefit plans dropped. We are beginning to feel the effects of that switch to defined contribution as the first wave of retirees roll out of their 401(k) plans. The timing of the DOL rule is perfect, because so many American workers need advice on generating income, not accumulating assets.

Planners who want to grow their business will need to reconcile the need to plan for income versus asset management. Clients will soon begin asking – if they aren't regularly doing so now – about how to generate income for life. The importance of asset management is decreasing, as evidenced by fee compression within the industry. Our clients simply do not see the value in asset allocation services the way they did during the accumulation phase of their lives.

Fee Disclosure

Many of us are already accustomed to disclosing fees. However, the change in client mentality will encourage us not only to disclose more often, but also redefine how we disclose. I sense that the new purpose of disclosure is more about understanding the client value and less about fees. Our clients are becoming more educated through unlimited educational resources, robo-advisors and fee-conscious service providers. Unfortunately, these trends are affecting the value of the traditional planner who focuses only on retirement income planning.

In the past, our fee structure included asset management. We now need to solidify how much is going for asset allocation services and how much is going to our other value-added services. Disclosure will force the successful planner to add more value. You might say that is simple fee compression, and it might be, but if you evolve into a holistic financial firm that offers more than just asset management, you have more justification for your fee structure. Those additional services can be added with scale and efficiency to replace or grow your revenue per client – now and in the future.

Re-engineered Marketing

Gaining clients in the future will be more difficult – even more difficult than it feels today. Our prospects have access to our backgrounds, our websites and our social media profiles within seconds. We are faced with so many chances to create one negative impression against hundreds of positive public interactions.

In the future, our prospects will come to our offices with more information about our firms than they ever had before. We, the planners, are at a disadvantage because we don't know as much about them. However, we can use technology to manage the marketing risks and turn them into a positive.

We must have a social media strategy with checks and balances – a process for posts and reviews. This will take effort to set up, but it will pay dividends in client acquisition. The costs associated with prospecting can become scalable and efficient if social media is used properly. Additionally, we should always be on the lookout for new ways to secure new clients using referrals and positive experiences.

While regulation will affect us in 2017, the financial planning marketplace is likely to have a more profound impact on how we grow going forward. Take the opportunity to evaluate how you will grow regardless of regulation.

Winning Strategy: Think about how changes in the market will affect your clients' views of retirement planning. Disclose your value differently than in the past, and focus on marketing those strengths in the future.

Success and Consistency

January 12, 2017

As many know, I'm a big college basketball fan. When you look at some of the most successful programs in the country, you'll find one thing in common: consistency in coaching. Coaches like Roy Williams at North

Carolina, Coach K at Duke, Bill Self at Kansas and Rick Pitino at Louisville have all been at their schools many years. Some years have been better than others at those schools, but no one can deny those programs have stamina and a level of excellence well above the average college program. Even with successful programs that have seen coaching changes over a period of years, the same culture will likely exist throughout the program.

Having a quality coach at the helm is equivalent to having consistency in your retirement portfolios. There will undoubtedly be market downturns and volatility, but consistency provides a powerful motivator for our clients to remain with their plans. Consistency comes from us always being in communication with our clients, especially in difficult market times. We must be a consistent voice for our clients and prospects, providing information, education and advice – even when our clients don't want to hear what we have to say. Plus, we need to listen and react to our clients' biggest concerns – turning their assets into retirement income.

Vehicles providing guaranteed income could create the kind of stamina and consistency in a portfolio our clients seek. It's not that the entire portfolio needs to be guaranteed – far from it. In fact, our research shows that between 18-28 percent of income should be guaranteed to optimize retirement. That leaves plenty of assets to be invested in an allocation strategy that can protect purchasing power due to inflation.

Our industry needs to look at new ways to provide guarantees and create consistency and stamina for retirement income. Several vehicles can reduce the pressure, or improve upon, a systematic withdrawal strategy. We need to educate our distributors, broker-dealers and advisors on vehicles like HECMs, income annuities and Qualified Longevity Annuity Contracts (QLACS). All are underutilized today but could provide valuable benefits to our clients' retirement income portfolios.

Winning Strategy: Think like a successful college program or sports franchise. Add consistency to your retirement income portfolios for more success with clients.

Think Like a Factory

January 19, 2017

I recently listened to a 30-minute podcast featuring Jeb Banner, CEO of Smallbox. Smallbox develops websites and consults on transformative ideas like putting employees first. The owner works with clients on Factory Days and/or Weeks. At their core, Factory Days are about reinvesting in yourself and your support staff.

Smallbox shut down its business for the first time in 2011 for a Factory Week, allowing everyone to get away from the business and work on themselves. Of course, we can all use time to improve ourselves – recuperate, recharge, relearn and discover new possibilities. Although the experiment was not perfect, it did focus on the employees and their development.

How often do you shut down your business to
improve your staff and your practice?

As planners, we control our schedules. Unfortunately, we allow our clients to set our weekly or daily schedules, and we tend to chase the "next case" or "next revenue source." We rarely take time to get off-site and work on our own practices. The old saying is "work on your business, not in it." I would say that most financial professionals are busy chasing the next urgent need, regardless of its importance. We simply love to be busy as a way of justifying our revenue to our clients. Worse yet, we have hired talented individuals to leverage our time, sales and service, but we don't always know how to use our staff in the most effective ways possible.

How much more balanced would your life be
if you didn't have to chase after every client need?

If you reinvest in your staff, I bet they will teach you a lot about your business. They will likely provide great ideas on becoming more efficient, providing better customer service and growing your business. But they need to know what to do and how to do it. A simple word for that process is "training." We rarely budget time, energy, dollars and other resources to make our staff members better. I'm almost certain that we all underutilize our sales support staff members. If we better train them, chances are we can have better balance in our lives – versus running around 10 to 12 hours a day.

Who do you think is most important?

While it may seem selfish, Smallbox argues that you and your staff are the most important assets you have. Ultimately, you are using your talents for the betterment of your clients' financial futures. However, you have to keep yourself and your staff engaged in ways that foster growth and improvement. Learning and growing allows you to provide more value to your clients and prospects. So, from time to time, take time to step away from your business and get re-engaged in your most important assets: you and your staff.

Winning Strategy: Schedule regular time throughout the year to think about your business, discover new ways to help clients and improve the skill sets of you and your staff. It's worth the investment.

The Future of Fees

January 26, 2017

Momentum continues to move toward the advisory business. I think there are two reasons for this. First, we have unprecedented potential regulation coming in April 2017, favoring advisory business with fees tied to assets under management. Second, we are seeing a continued industry shift to more passive investments and lower cost models – both of which force advisors to use the lower fee structures found in advisory models.

Many industry experts expect those fees to continue to be driven down over the next 24-36 months due to regulation and market forces. I agree.

So, how can we prove our value to our clients and prospects and protect our revenue while working in the best interests of our clients? Below are a couple of ideas I think successful planners should attend to, now and in the future, not only to maintain their practice, but also grow it!

Fee Transparency

I'm not talking about simply telling clients how much we charge for our services. That has become a given because of regulation. And, more importantly, market forces – not the U.S. Department of Labor (DOL) – will make all our fees for services look very similar. So transparency will likely differentiate successful planners in the future.

It's appropriate to charge 25-40 basis points for assets under management and disclose that amount. It's also appropriate to charge another 40 basis points for comprehensive planning with annual monitoring and/or quarterly reviews. And it's appropriate to charge a certain level of basis points when planning for protection-related issues – longevity, death, disability and chronic illnesses.

Vibrant Protection Platform

With an emphasis on passive investments coming from the DOL, it will be harder to justify a high fee structure for clients when our services are limited to asset management. Absent of active managers, you might be setting yourself up for unhappy clients when you disclose the value of the fee. Having a protection platform will be critical for future success.

Our clients' No. 1 fear remains outliving their money, and half of Americans underestimate their life expectancy. Talking about contingencies and mitigating those risks will be paramount in the new financial planning world. You need a team capable of executing on complex insurance and longevity issues in order to protect your assets under management and have any chance of retaining those assets with the next generation.

Collaborate

From the first time I read the DOL rule, I have said that most planners need to come to grips with two questions:

1. Am I going to move up market?

2. If I stay in my current market, how do I become more efficient and capture market share?

Our industry is one of the most collaborative I have ever seen. We are willing to share clients for the good of the client. Our clients have complicated issues that require expertise in many specialties. Therefore, we must bring experts to the table for our clients. We need to have a quarterback mentality to not only direct and execute a financial plan, but also bring in experts to have the most success.

That coordination of talent, expertise and access is valuable to our clients. Having a network can bring value on top of your specialty, which may soon be subject to fee compression.

I can go on and on about changes in fee structure and the impact of regulation, but I think you get the idea – we have to look for different ways to earn our revenue from clients. That means we need to expand our services to platforms we haven't been offering to date, including life insurance, guaranteed income and chronic illness protection. Our clients will rightly expect a full accounting of our fee structure. Being able to clearly outline the value they receive will make it easier to have the fee conversation.

Winning Strategy: Don't look at disclosure as a reason to reduce fees because the market is reducing its fee. Value will be important in the future. We simply need to redefine our value, change our practices to offer important services to our prospects and be transparent in the fee structure.

The Fixed or Indexed Decision

February 2, 2017

In 2016, we experienced a large rise in the sale of fixed annuities. This makes some sense as we moved through an uncertain political landscape in a falling interest rate environment ... clients were looking for safety and guarantees. However, the use of fixed indexed annuities can provide the same safety and produce similar, if not better, returns than a traditional fixed annuity.

Our office took a look at the past 30 years of returns of a fixed indexed annuity – using current cap rates – and compared the returns from a multiyear fixed rate annuity. The results surprised me. With a 5.25 percent cap rate in years 1-4, a 5 percent cap rate in years 5-6, and a 4.75 percent cap rate after that, we compared the seven-year accumulation values against a 2.85 percent guaranteed return over the same period. More than 93 percent of the periods over the past 30 years resulted in a higher fixed indexed annuity value than the 2.85 percent guarantee.

When the fixed rate did exceed the FIA accumulation, the difference was only an average of $288 over the seven-year period. When the FIA's accumulation was higher, the average gain over the fixed rate was $7,876 over the seven-year period. While the risk exists that the client may have zero interest credited during a period when the index had no gains, history tells us there is a 93 percent chance the client will have more value with a FIA versus a fixed-rate instrument, given today's rates.

Even better, we are seeing the use of advisory-based FIAs emerge in the marketplace. Due to the lack of commission built into the product, cap rates are substantially higher. However, even with a 75 basis points fee assumed in the analysis, there was a 100 percent historical precedent that the FIA outperformed the interest rate. Too often, we look at fixed annuities or bonds to balance our equity risk or remove interest rate risk. The FIA can provide the same protection and higher potential returns if the client is willing to risk the small guaranteed rate. In forgoing that guarantee, the client maintains principal protection and higher potential yields.

It's time to re-look at FIAs as a part of the portfolio and not just sell what is easy. Instead, let's take time to educate our clients on the value and potential benefits of owning a FIA, which can provide access to downside protection, no interest rate fluctuations, guaranteed income and tax-deferred growth (assuming nonqualified assets). Historically, your client is in a better position to earn a higher accumulation value over a typical seven-year surrender period. Take the time to look at an alternative to bonds for a portion of your clients' portfolios.

Winning Strategy: Research shows that the accumulation values in FIAs have outpaced multiyear guaranteed fixed-rate annuities. Take time to look at alternatives that can better your client portfolios.

Important Demographic Shifts

February 9, 2017

One of my presentations focuses on demographic changes in the United States over the last 20 years – changes that will likely impact the retirement income space for several decades.

Some changes are the costs associated with increased longevity. Others are the rate of savings in the United States, which has been declining since the late 1970s, resulting in smaller asset values to work with as we seek to generate future income. But, I think the one change not discussed enough is the shift from defined benefit to defined contribution plans we have seen over the past 20 years.

Defined contribution plans continue to grow in popularity due to the large selection of funds, lower costs and tax advantages. But few plans have access to guaranteed income like a defined benefit plan. Only recently have 401(k) plans begun to add deferred-income annuities to some target date selections. In our research at Ash Brokerage, we find that a portfolio can be optimized (a 95 percent chance of one dollar left in the portfolio at age 95) with somewhere between 18-25 percent of the portfolio in guaranteed income. Guaranteed income may be Social Security, pension or annuities.

When I talk with plan sponsors about their retirement benefits for employees, I find a ton of information in their offices about risk tolerance tests, asset allocation and fund performance. But I rarely see or hear intelligent, meaningful conversations about converting this wealth into income. The loss of guaranteed income streams provided by pension plans places additional pressure on our remaining assets to generate income.

The shift away from defined benefit plans seems to have shifted the attention of our asset managers as well. Too many of our pension plans are currently underfunded. Some plans are just as insolvent as the Social Security system. Many plans have invested in significant bond holdings. In a potentially rising interest rate environment, this can be devastating. As more baby boomers with these frozen pension plans inch closer to accessing their income, many plans will see increased pressure on funding levels as payouts increase and bond prices decrease.

This demographic change can open an opportunity for those planners who address it. Talking to your clients about getting in position for retirement income now can put planners in a leadership role with their clients. Giving clients the option of guaranteed income will likely provide stability to the portfolio and peace of mind. Although this shift will end up being costly to most consumers, the financial planning industry can step in and provide proper strategies to many Americans.

Winning Strategy: Understand how consumer behavior over the last two decades will impact retirement income planning. More income from fewer assets, less guaranteed income available from employer plans and increased longevity risks can provide opportunities to expand your value proposition to the client.

Advantages in the Uncertainty of Rates

February 16, 2017

The 10-year Treasury has jumped nearly 75 basis points since Donald Trump's election. If you talk with some economists, they'll say the rate increase will continue; others predict a softening of rates back to the average over the past three years. The Fed has indicated they would like to see rates above 3 percent by 2019. In reality, we simply do not know where rates are going – short-term or long-term.

So, what should you do with your clients in an uncertain rate environment? I suggest you take advantage of this uncertainty and talk to your clients about how to properly mitigate interest rate risks – now and in the future. As rates were falling in the first half of 2016, we saw a significant increase in five-year, multiyear guarantee annuity sales. Advisors were trying to lock in clients for a period of time while the 10-year Treasury fell precipitously throughout the first six months of the year. However, we need to take advantage of the time to change the conversation with interest rates.

Instead of reacting to rate changes and chasing the rate environment, try to begin repositioning the interest-driven portion of your portfolio for success, regardless of the rate environment. I think this can best be done using the concept of laddering, a viable tactic to take advantage of any rate environment. It's a simple move that places your financial vehicles at different maturities over a certain time frame.

Once the short-term vehicle matures, you reposition it to the longest maturity available. When the next shortest-term instrument matures, you reposition it for the same long-term maturity. After going through your initial investments, you have laddered your portfolio.

The result of doing this creates liquidity and better rates. Your client is now positioned with all the interest-driven assets at the longest portion of the yield curve – the part with the historically highest rates and yields. At the same time, you have a steady source of cash if the client needs liquidity.

By positioning a pocket of money in a ladder annually, the client has liquidity to a portion of their portfolio each year. If the client believes more will be needed, simply position a larger percentage in each pocket of money and, perhaps, shorten the long-term maturity. A lower yield is the likely cost of more liquidity.

Thinking about long-term solutions for interest rate risk is sorely needed now – not because of a rising interest rate risk but because we must move away from transaction-based solutions. Your clients will appreciate the value you have added to the relationship with an actual solution versus worrying about an uncontrollable event such as a change in interest rates.

Winning Strategy: Look at laddering the fixed income portion of your portfolio regardless of financial vehicle. Putting your clients in the highest yield position with liquidity requires some repositioning but makes sense now and in the future.

Simplicity in Business

February 23, 2017

I've been traveling this past week to several different conferences, and I have already picked up some great ideas to share with our advisors. Through my travels, I was struck by a couple of comments about the simplicity and authenticity of business. I'm always surprised about how the simplest and most direct statements are often the most valuable.

I had the great honor of speaking at The Society of Financial Service Professionals (FSP) Arizona Institute. As I was preparing for the event, I remembered that the FSP played a large part in one of the largest sales during my retail career. After receiving a large lump sum of money that increased their net worth, a couple had a question about college funding and the eligibility of future assistance. College funding and financial assistance were not my areas of expertise, so I sent my question to the discussion board at the association and received a lot of valuable information in return.

I was able to discuss the case with another professional with expertise in financial assistance and planning, and I passed along that information to my client. The knowledge I passed along from that source added value to my interactions with my prospective client. I also encouraged the couple to contact my source if they felt the need to explore additional information. Because of my relationship with a network of professionals, I was able to add value beyond my expertise. The couple elected my firm to manage their money due to my ability to look holistically at their current situation.

Added value – value that is important to the person you are working with – can come in many flavors. As I was sitting in a carrier meeting this week, I was reminded about the simplicity of business when you work on bringing value to the relationship. The speaker commented on three things that make you successful in business, regardless of your industry:

1. People like you.

2. People trust you.

3. You add value. If you add value, it's easier to get people to like and trust you.

So simple. So right. But too often ignored. This simple checklist for business relationships resonated with me. Our value to our clients will be the knowledge and wisdom we bring to the relationship. We are quickly moving to business models that require technology to make investment selections and recommendations. However, our clients will still require value in the form of personal expertise, a trusting relationship and the ability to have a meaningful conversation.

We have to find the proper expansion of our business models to add value. With one of the greatest fears of Americans still being running out of money in retirement, I suggest we take a hard look at the longevity issues around income planning. This can easily add value to your relationships and provide a means to have a unique conversation with your clients and prospects.

Winning Strategy: Take a look at the simple aspects of your client relationships. Leverage your likability, trust and value propositions to recruit new clients.

Part II

Delays, Distractions and Disturbances

DOL Issues Proposed Delay

March 2, 2017

Today, the U.S. Department of Labor (DOL) posted a proposed delay to its fiduciary and conflicts of interest rule on the Federal Register. The delay pushes the applicability date to June 9, 2017, which amounts to a 60-day delay to the rule. This is significantly less than what many industry professionals hoped for after President Donald Trump's memorandum Feb. 3, 2017.

As the fiduciary rule continues to evolve, I want to stress that many aspects of the rule have already been implemented in the marketplace. Firms have created policies and procedures to mitigate the conflicts in their business and supervise best interest standards for clients. Advisors have begun to change their business models to adhere to the new rules. All of these movements are positives for our industry, and we look forward to continue delivering products, services, strategies and solutions to our advisors in a neutral, conflict-free environment.

Looking into a foggy crystal ball, our industry must accept that the rule – in some form – seems to be inevitable. How the rule is supervised and executed will ultimately change the distribution of retirement products forever. I want to encourage all members of the financial services community to stay engaged with their senators and representatives in shaping the DOL rule. Ultimately, I believe a legislative fiduciary standard is the best outcome to unify the standard across all distribution channels and geographic markets. The standard must work with NAIC regulations that govern fixed and indexed annuities, while outlining a centralized regulator to hold all professionals accountable.

Ash Brokerage continues to prepare for the fiduciary and conflicts of interest rule. As we inch closer to a resolution, we will work with our independent agents to ensure they have an avenue with the least amount of disruption to their business. For our registered representatives and registered investment advisors, we are prepared to support and assist you in the transition to a new environment. Our tools, research and expertise working in an agnostic sales organization provide the necessary support for success in the future. We look forward to partnering with firms and advisors who are preparing to thrive in the new world of delivering retirement products and services to so many Americans who need our advice.

What You Can Do While We Wait for Answers on the DOL

March 9, 2017

Since Feb. 3, when the president signed a memorandum asking the U.S. Department of Labor to review the fiduciary and conflicts of interest rule, I've talked to agents and advisors from around the county. Many feel a great sense of relief that the rule is likely to be delayed – many believe this is the beginning of the end for the rule.

Regardless of any delay or revision, I don't believe we can afford to move backward in how we interact with our clients. The fiduciary standard is here to stay – market forces and regulatory agencies already act as if the rule is in effect.

I think it's vital to prepare for running your office as if you are a fiduciary. While we wait for answers on the DOL, you can set yourself up for success by taking a few key steps:

1. **Review your sales process.** Make it repeatable and document it. Think about how you interact with your clients. Document

every step, and turn it into a policy and procedure manual for client interaction. The final product is less important if you follow a consistent process.

2. **Evaluate your vendors.** Whether it's software, fact finding, brokerage agencies or broker-dealers, are they able to support your business model and help you execute what best supports your client base and growth plans?

3. **Get comfortable with transparency in fees.** Most clients will appreciate your plans to remain in the business and continue to stay in contact with them. Don't be afraid to discuss your model and thoughts around compensation.

4. **Listen to your clients.** Engage with them however best meets their needs. I don't believe any business model is superior to another so long as your engagement is defined by client need.

5. **Think about your compensation** – in relation to time, effort, expertise and what the client is asking to get accomplished. Concentrate on neutrality when defining your fees with a group of clients.

These are just the beginning steps to prepare for a fiduciary standard – they represent the fundamental building blocks. As planners, we can't defer our fiduciary responsibility any further. Instead, we should look at this possible delay as an opportunity to refine our practice and enhance our client experience.

Winning Strategy: Take time to prepare for a fiduciary standard. If there is a delay in the DOL rule, you can get your business in a better position for success. Make fiduciary a positive differentiator for you as you look to thrive in our new marketplace.

Why You Need to Change Your Game

March 16, 2017

Last year, I heard Robbie Bach speak at a carrier meeting. His story stuck with me – it might stick with you, too, and inspire you to change your business model for a post-fiduciary world.

If you've never heard of Robbie, he's the former leader of Microsoft's Mobile Entertainment and Device division and was responsible for developing and bringing Xbox to the market. The console was eventually a success but at one point, Robbie thought about resigning. He'd lost nearly $6 billion and was unable to penetrate the Japanese gaming market.

To better fit his market's wants and desires, Robbie created an interactive, subscription-based business model. For a set price per year, players could not only access Microsoft's games, but they could also see and hear the other players around the globe via headsets and cameras. No other game allowed that level of interaction before.

The results were outstanding. In a short period of time, Robbie's division went from billions in losses to a $1 billion profit. Even more impressive was their penetration of the Japanese market – Xbox earned a nearly 10 percent market share when no one had been able to earn more than 1 percent. His tweak in the business model and addition of value created a sustainable growth trajectory for the division.

What's Your Game Plan?

In the post-fiduciary world, a proper business model will be critical to your success. I think it's the biggest decision you'll have to make as you prepare for the move toward a fiduciary-based practice.

You'll need to either move up market, or become more efficient in your current market. Neither option is right or wrong – you just need to be crystal clear in your decision.

- **If you move up market,** how will you address the concerns and needs of higher net worth clients? Wealthy individuals tend to have access to better health care, so their longevity needs will be different.

Wealth transfer and taxes may be a bigger part of their planning process. Is your model set up to deliver those types of services as a holistic package?

- **If you stay in your current market,** how is it changing? Industry reports indicate more than $600 billion in assets will shake free from large wire houses and banks that have less than $100,000 in account values. That's a lot of assets you could capture, but efficiency will be critical to success. Do you have the right vendors for technology, software and applications to deliver products and services to these clients?

Winning Strategy: Review your business model and make sure it sets you up for success. No model is superior to another, but the model you choose has to be right for you and your clients.

Winning the Right Way

March 23, 2017

If you read much about the U.S. Department of Labor (DOL) fiduciary rule, you know many people are saying it's unworkable. While I agree the rule may be overreaching and it will be difficult to meet all the disclosure requirements, I think it's clear the effects of the rule are making a difference already. FINRA has fined an institution for creating conflicts and incentives to sell one product, and clients are asking prospective planners if they are a fiduciary.

Still, many advisors feel like they cannot work as a fiduciary. I believe with the right focus, you can.

Defining Success

As an Indiana University student manager, I worked in one of the most competitive environments in college basketball. We didn't always win. In fact, my sophomore year was one of the worst in Indiana's history under Coach Bob Knight. Two years later, we were ranked in the top 10 in many of the polls throughout the season, and we won the national title.

Coach Knight eventually retired as the winning-est coach in NCAA history with 902 wins. His teams won three NCAA titles, one NIT championship, and 11 Big Ten conference titles, and he won numerous Coach of the Year awards – those are the accolades most people remember him for. But, I think it's important to recognize to more stats:

- Coach Knight graduated 98 percent of his student-athletes who stepped foot on campus
- He had ZERO NCAA violations during his four-decades-long coaching career

Success in sports is usually defined in wins and losses, awards, titles and rankings. But at Indiana, we were taught that the real win is how you play the game and how you improve your chances for success beyond basketball.

I find our charge as financial planners very similar. Our industry has to pay attention to how we handle clients, improve their chances for success and help them enjoy their retirement in the event of major longevity issues. We have to be more cognizant of the process we use with clients and how we plan.

The DOL rule is meant to protect retirement investors, but it should really be about redefining our practices. The successful planner in a post-fiduciary world will have a process that:

- Addresses the many risks of retirement
- Makes interaction feel unique to the client
- Promotes the sharing of information at lightning-fast response times

That is not unworkable with a growing, caring and thriving financial services business.

Winning Strategy: Take a page from a legendary coach. Focus on the process – not the results. Redefine how you interact with your clients and make their experience unique. You can win by staying within the rules and focusing on what's important.

Resting on the Red Sweater: How You Can Be as Calm as Bob Knight Before the Big Game

March 30, 2017

March Madness is the most exciting time of the year for me – even more exciting than Christmas. You see, this time of year always brings back memories of Indiana's run to the national championship in 1987.

As a student manager, I can remember preparing the bench for the national championship game at the Superdome in New Orleans, Louisiana. I was extremely anxious – everyone was. And, as I walked back into our locker room for the last time before warm-ups, what I saw made me even more anxious.

Coach Bob Knight was laying on the training table. He'd folded his famous red sweater into a nice, neat pillow … I couldn't believe he seemed to be resting peacefully just minutes before our biggest game of the year.

Looking back now, however, I think he was at peace because he knew our team was prepared. During the season, we had several days to prepare for games, but for the national championship, we had just 48 hours. However, we followed the exact same process:

- The team reviewed the players from Syracuse right after the national semifinal
- The coaches watched film Saturday night and presented the game plan to the players the following morning
- On game day, we went through the exact same preparations as we did for every other game in the season
- We continued to use our model of basketball – man-to-man defense and motion offense

Preparing for Your Own Big Game

When it comes to preparing for the fiduciary rule, you can use the same formula for success. As planners, most of us already act and make recommendations in the best interest of our clients. However, we need to document our sales process and make it repeatable.

Though the outcome was different for each game, the Hoosiers' process remained consistent through the 1987 season. We evaluated each team's strengths and weaknesses from top to bottom – we didn't just look at the team's starting five or star players.

Similarly, as planners, we have to focus on all the risks associated with financial planning. Too often, we look at asset management as the solution to wealth management. But, we also have to consider longevity needs (so our clients don't run out of money), long-term care, taxes, the death of a spouse and transferring their legacy to the next generation. These concerns need to be evaluated as a regular part of our client process.

I encourage everyone to evaluate their sales and business practices during the time remaining before the fiduciary rule takes effect. You could say it's already in effect due to many broker-dealers implementing new strategies and FINRA assessing fines based on conflicts of interest. To reduce your risk of litigation, you should prepare to win, and prepare consistently.

Winning Strategy: Establish a sales process that is repeatable and easily documented. Consistency will allow you to focus on your clients' needs, and it will force you to consider all the risks.

Rule Delay Announced

April 5, 2017

In two days, the U.S. Department of Labor (DOL) will likely publish an official delay of its fiduciary and conflicts of interest rule. Many in our industry have been waiting for this rule to be delayed, but several points around the fiduciary rule remain uncertain. Industry experts predict a further delay, allowing the DOL to fully complete President Donald Trump's requested review of the rule.

I want to stress to all who work in our industry that many aspects of the rule will go into effect June 9, 2017. Most notably, impartial conduct standards must be adhered to on any qualified sale after the delayed implementation date. Although the Best Interest Contract (BIC) requirement appears to be have been pushed off until Jan. 1, 2018, the sale of an annuity inside a qualified account must be in the best interest of the client, make no misleading statements and have reasonable compensation tied to the transaction.

More importantly, our industry has already begun to shift to the fiduciary status and will continue to do so before the June 9 delayed implementation date. For those of us serving clients, it continues to be table stakes to work in the best interest of our clients. We must work toward the standard of care that every client deserves while protecting our profession that serves those clients.

Even with the relief of the BIC through 2017, we need to look at the next nine months as an opportunity to evolve in the fiduciary world. We must continue to evaluate our sales process, our product shelves and the holistic nature of our clients' needs. The successful retirement advisor of the future will get to the fiduciary standard quicker, work more efficiently and be more effective with each client.

Ash Brokerage stands committed to helping all our advisors make this transition. As implementation grows clearer in the coming weeks and months, we will announce several tools and resources to help you.

Many aspects of the rule remain unanswered. Namely, the independent marketing organization exemption continues through the review process without finalized thresholds for marketing organizations to sign the BIC in 2018. We look forward to continue being part of the conversation in shaping these important changes to our industry. Look for continued information through Ash's sales teams and social media. I look forward to growth in our industry with the increased care that the rule will provide to our clients.

Be Ready for the Questions Your Clients Will Be Asking

April 6, 2017

As I was traveling around the country attending conferences, The New York Times published an article that caught the attention of many people in our industry. "The 21 Questions You're Going To Need To Ask About Investment Fees" points out questions we all need to get comfortable answering.* Better yet, we should prepare to discuss them upfront with our clients

The article is a perfect example of the market effects taking place in the financial services industry. While the U.S. Department of Labor fiduciary rule has been delayed, our industry has already started a transition that is unlikely to be reversed. Our clients have been exposed to many of the perceived conflicts that exist in our business, and they have the right to ask appropriate questions.

At the same time, I believe it is entirely appropriate to continue selling commission-based products, especially in long-term income planning and tax-deferral situations. Simple math indicates that commission-based products, when used properly, enhance the client position in many cases (as with any product solution).

The article asks questions about compensation, incentives, trips and fees. All of these are important to disclose to our clients in the future. If incentives are involved, I would argue we need to be upfront about those in the new fiduciary world. In fact, we need to figure a way to not be incentivized and focus on vendors making our business more efficient and effective. In the end, we must be prepared to answer all our clients' questions about our compensation, the fees of the product and why the particular product is the proper solution.

As an industry, we need to take this type of article to heart. The news media should not be educating our clients about fiduciary status. Instead, we need to show them how valuable financial service professionals can be in building a long-term retirement and wealth management plan. If we commit to that, everyone wins.

Winning Strategy: Whom do you want educating your clients – you and your staff or the news media? Stay ahead of any hype. Be ready to answer questions about fees and compensation.

New York Times, "The 21 Questions You're Going to Need to Ask About Investment Fees," Feb. 10, 2017: https://www.nytimes.com/2017/02/10/your-money/the-21-questions-youre-going-to-need-to-ask-about-investment-fees.html?_r=0

Add Value or Become Extinct
April 13, 2017

We've been talking about the market forces within the financial services industry that are moving us toward a new fiduciary environment. Even though the U.S. Department of Labor fiduciary rule is delayed until summer, what started in late 2016 continues to gain momentum.

What We've Already Seen

At the end of last year, several firms announced strategies to mitigate conflicts of interest, and news articles have been urging consumers to ask their advisor if they are a fiduciary. Several advisors have told me that prospects have asked them on the phone if they are fiduciaries before making an appointment.

It is clear that changes in our business began even before the rule was announced. According to Morningstar, the number of exchange-traded funds charging less than 10 basis points rose from 125 to 348 from 2010 to 2015.* Consumers have more access to information than ever before, and more groups are focused on the educational aspects of our industry, which is a good thing for everyone. So, even though the rule, the delay and the pending litigation remain a focal point for our industry, consumer groups are already forcing change.

What's to Come

It seems compressed revenue, whether it be fee- or commission-based, will likely take hold over the next three to five years. If you are only earning revenue from managing assets, you need to rethink your business model. Some experts believe asset management only will gross only 40-50 basis points, and we clearly see the trend moving that way.

What You Need to Do

To sustain a healthy business model as a planner, you'll need to expand your horizon and modify how you manage wealth. That includes leveraging protection solutions, such as insurance, annuities and alternative products, to maximize your client relationships. Many of us many will need to partner or merge with experts in collaborating fields in order to grow revenues. Without a doubt, you'll need to add valuable services that will retain customers and help you acquire new relationships.

If you stagnate in your offerings, you will likely find yourself earning less than the 40-50 basis points mentioned. Or, you might find yourself out of business.

Your clients will only continue to become more fee-conscious and look for the most efficient asset management. There's too much information out there about asset allocation services, so that can't be your only offering. Instead, your expertise should be driving from managing different and expanded segments of your clients' financial lives. But that will require a willingness, a mindset, a toughness and a curiosity to make your clients' lives better in the long run. I'm confident all of us in the financial professional community are up to the challenge.

Winning Strategy: Look to add to your existing services in order to offset the likely fee- or commission-based compression over the next three to five years. Adding valuable solutions to your menu of client services will provide leverage and lift future revenue in your firm.

*Wall Street Journal, "WSJ Wealth Adviser Briefing: Broker Fee War, Morgan's Make-Right, FAs on Snap's IPO," March 1, 2017: http://blogs.wsj.com/moneybeat/2017/03/01/wsj-wealth-adviser-briefing-broker-fee-war-morgans-make-right-fas-on-snaps-ipo/

QLACs: The Unused Gift

April 20, 2017

In 2014, the U.S. Treasury Department released new rules around Qualified Longevity Annuity Contracts (QLACs). After an initial increase in utilization, the focus and attention dwindled over the past two years. Today, the sale of all deferred income annuities remains stagnant and far below expectations from 2014. This gift from the government remains largely unused in the planning community.

As I prepared for a presentation recently, I asked our team to update our research on the use of QLACs at different ages and for different risk allocation models. The results were similar to an earlier study we did in 2015. In fact, the results from 2017 are even more convincing for the use of QLACs.

Keep in mind the interest rate environment hasn't changed significantly over the past 24 months, yet a fixed instrument was proven to improve the probability of success across many categories. With such a wide improvement, we owe it to our clients to consider this solution in the retirement planning process.

A Closer Look

Our QLAC study evaluated four asset allocation models:

- Aggressive – 80/20 equity-bond allocation
- Moderate-aggressive – 60/40 allocation
- Moderate-conservative – 40/60 allocation
- Conservative – 20/80 allocation

The initial investment started at ages 55, 60, 65 and 70. We looked at placing a $500,000 portfolio in each of the allocations. Each portfolio began a reasonable distribution of income beginning at age 70. For each allocation strategy, there was a probability of having $1 left in the portfolio at ages 90, 95 and 100.

Next, we placed a QLAC at each one of those ages and allocation strategies. The annuity began paying out at age 80. With QLACs, you tend to change income start dates five years before and after the initial requested start date – this gives the client a 10-year window if their needs change. So, there are 48 results cells between ages 55, 60, 65 and 70 in the four different allocation strategies when we look at longevity at 90, 95 and 100.

In every one of those 48 cells, the study found that a QLAC improved the probability of success. What surprised me was the fact that some of the largest improvements in success rates happened when a QLAC was purchased at younger ages.

A Change in Mindset

Too often, we think of QLACs as a way to push required minimum distributions down the road. Instead, we need to initiate a conversation about this solution in order to mitigate the risk of longevity. In doing so, we reduce some of the concerns our clients have about running out of income during their life. We clearly help some of our younger, more conservative clients in the process.

Winning Strategy: Take time to evaluate the use of deferred income annuities in the planning process with clients. Their best interests might be served by providing guaranteed income later in life. Our study shows that you can engage a client and have a high probability of helping them improve their retirement outcomes.

Vision for What Your Effort Will Deliver

April 27, 2017

A couple of weeks ago, I was talking with my business coach, CJ McClanahan, and he said something that struck me: "People don't have a vision for what the effort is going to deliver." If you think about that statement, it applies to several parts of our lives as financial planners.

Vision for Your Practice

In today's increasingly regulated environment, we tend to focus our attention on fighting the U.S. Department of Labor rule. In practice, the rule has already taken effect as clients are already asking planners if they are fiduciaries. For the last nine months, banks and wire houses have been converting their clients, for better or worse, to fee-based accounts. And, as I travel around the country, I hear too many people talking about what they are going to do to fight the rule, rather than what they are going to do to implement the rule in their practice.

The rule will undoubtedly require a lot of effort to fully implement, but our clients are likely to benefit from the changes that the rule suggests. Putting our clients' best interests first has always been a part of our ethical makeup. However, the documentation needed to prove this status will require changing how we process our client files, complete our paperwork and follow our sales process.

That said, we tend to lack the vision of what our businesses may be like when we implement the rule. Your clients will likely have more trust in you. They will likely discuss more concerns with you. And, they will be more likely to refer you to other like-minded prospects. Those items can make your business more profitable and more efficient.

Vision for Your Clients

At the same time, our clients lack vision in the financial planning process. Most clients spend more time planning this year's vacation than they do planning their retirement. We have to do a better job of providing that vision through education and motivating them to complete the planning process.

Without a doubt, the planning process can be onerous if done properly. Planning should consider all the risks of retirement, including longevity, legacy and charitable desires, taxes and health care, to mention a few. Each of those risks needs special consideration, evaluation and analysis to prepare a proper recommendation for each client's concerns, goals and objectives.

Few people want to think about those risks, let alone plan for them or act upon them. It's our job as financial professionals to create a positive vision of the outcomes for our clients: sustainable retirement income, better lifestyle management and more time with children and grandchildren.

Eyes on the Prize

In the end, vision becomes an important part of the planning process and our business models. We must keep the vision of all changes in perspective, but we must also envision the benefits of change. In doing so, we can easily put forth the efforts needed today for a better business and happier client relationships.

Winning Strategy: Few people maintain the vision of the effort required in order to improve amidst change. That applies to clients and planners. Take time to think about where your clients need to be in the future and where your business needs to be in three to five years. Keep that vision in the front of your mind for proper motivation to change.

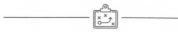

Longevity and Golf

May 4, 2017

The title might make you think that I will be talking about how to spend your retirement years. Without a doubt, many people spend more time driving a golf cart around the course, or their neighborhood for that matter, during retirement. However, longevity and golf share other commonalities in the retirement income space.

In 2016, Dustin Johnson was at the top of the money list for the PGA Tour, earning more than $9.3 million.* (This does not account for his endorsements, just his winnings from the 22 tournaments he played in 2016.) One of the reasons he won so often or ended close to the top of the leader board when he played was his putts per hole. For the entire season, Dustin Johnson putted 1.71 times per golf hole.

The 100th best PGA golfer for 2016, Adam Hadwin, earned $1,067,809 – just 11.4 percent of what Dustin earned for the same season. Adam played in slightly more tournaments throughout the year, too. His putting average was 1.77 putts per hole … just 0.06 strokes more. But that little difference in putting made an $8.2 million difference in income.

Fortunately for Adam, he has a chance to learn from his experience, and he will likely earn more throughout the rest of his career. In fact, in 2017, he has already won a tournament and matched his previous year's income.

Sink Your Putts

Unfortunately, our clients don't get the same opportunity to rebound in retirement. Instead, they make largely irrevocable decisions when they leave their working years, so they have to get it right the first time. Like putting, the smallest movements can have huge consequences.

We must guide our clients through the complexities of longevity. A major health event that requires home health care or skilled nursing might demolish the assets a person has saved. And, simply living too long creates added stress on their ability to keep pace with inflation. All are real problems that, for the most part, must be dealt with when your clients stop working and start living off their accumulated assets.

Minor tweaks like asset allocation may improve or lessen a portfolio's ability to sustain itself through a systematic spend down over the rest of a retiree's life. You should take time to learn about new techniques and products for your clients. With new risks surrounding longevity and retirement income planning in general, you owe it to your clients to be innovative, creative and purposeful in your planning. Just like practicing your putting, practicing your profession can make a big difference for your clients and prospects.

Winning Strategy: Keep current with new products and strategies to give your clients the best opportunity for success. When you concentrate on the small things you can tweak, you will likely have profound improvements in your clients' retirement success.

PGA Tour Official Money Board, 2016: http://www.pgatour.com/stats/stat.109.2016.html

Longevity for Your Practice

May 11, 2017

You likely spend a lot of time talking about the importance of longevity planning for your clients. But, have you thought about longevity for your practice?

Recently, I read an article from a practice management expert who answered some questions about an advisor's succession planning. It made me think about how prepared we are as an industry to provide ongoing service to our clients in the event of catastrophic events. We talk to our clients about mitigating risks in retirement, but we don't necessarily talk about the risk of losing an advisor.

I think it's an important topic for us to consider, especially now. Part of working in your clients' best interests might include having a strategy for your office to make sure you continue servicing your clients after you leave the business – by your own choice or due to an external event. Think about how you would feel if you put your entire trust into a relationship with someone, and then that person suddenly left. Wouldn't you feel better if you knew there was a plan in place to continue taking care of you?

Sound Familiar?

This article focused on several mid-50s principals who did not have official succession plans. Children were going to step into the businesses if a health event forced the principals out; however, neither the staff nor the clients were aware of these plans. The children probably were not aware of the plans either, given that they had successful careers elsewhere. Unfortunately, this scenario is common among financial professionals.

With our clients in focus, we must have better plans for our retirement – which might come tomorrow due to a health event, or in a few years due to a simple desire to slow down. Regardless of timing, you owe it to your clients to give thought to the consequences. You also owe it to your employees, your families and the industry.

Look in the mirror and ask yourself, "Have I created a holistic plan for the orderly transition of my business? And, is it up to date?" If not, you need to devote time and energy to helping yourself first, so you can help more clients and prospects with confidence.

Winning Strategy: Think about how you will exit the business. What would your clients think if you were not at your firm tomorrow or the next day? You need to plan for the orderly transition of your business so you can instill confidence in your clients and staff.

Racing Toward Retirement Success

May 18, 2017

When you grow up in Indianapolis, you naturally follow racing to some degree. I'm not a huge racing fan, but I do follow the sport. (Actually, I follow just about any sport that offers an opportunity to make an analogy with our industry.)

As Memorial Day and the 101st running of the Indianapolis 500 approaches, I thought I'd share some statistics from the first race of this year's IndyCar Series.

In the Firestone Grand Prix of St. Petersburg, the winning margin was just 10 seconds. Now, on a race track, 10 seconds may seem like a massive win for the first-place car. But, think about how narrow that margin really is over the entire race, when things could have gone wrong at any point ...

- There were 110 laps with multiple turns both right and left
- The teams had to complete three pit stops
- The drivers had to make hundreds of gear shifts

The timing of all of the above had to be near perfect in order to win because the next competitor was just 10 seconds behind. With any loss in momentum, the driver could have easily lost the race.

Winning the Retirement Race

Just as anything can happen in 100-plus laps of an IndyCar race, you can never know what to expect in a 20 to 30-year retirement span. Both inflation and long-term care pose serious risks to our clients' plans. Without a strong plan and skilled execution, they could easily be thrown off track.

Our clients need to think about all the twists and turns retirement might bring, and we need to make sure their incomes don't lose momentum. We need to make sure they're able to finish strong. QLACs, deferred income annuities, income riders and hybrid long-term care plans are just a few of the recent innovations that allow us to help our clients complete the race. Because in their race, it's either first ... or last.

Winning Strategy: Look at ways to protect your clients from inflation and longevity concerns. Clients have to complete a long race that includes dangerous turns, a few pit stops and the need to maintain momentum for the long haul.

Why You Should Be Optimistic About the Future

May 25, 2017

While you might be afraid of the fiduciary rule and its effects on your business, there are so many reasons to be optimistic about the future of our profession right now. Below is a list of just a few of the changes I believe will continue to impact our industry – and increase the need for quality financial professionals – for years to come.

Defined Contribution Plans: Defined contribution plans offer better choices, potentially lower fees and tax-favored investing. However, few plans have mechanisms to provide lifetime income, so the vast majority of Americans need advice on converting their accumulated wealth into sustainable income. The loss of guaranteed income places pressure on assets under management like never before. The planner who specializes in income planning will differentiate themselves for decades to come.

Savings Rates: For long-term retirement savings, the savings rate in the United States remains around 5 percent, and baby boomers have a median retirement account balance of $130,100, according to LIMRA's 2016 Retirement Fact Book.[1] This means as planners, we will be challenged to generate more income with fewer assets than ever before. Clients will value creative and innovative professionals much more than a computer program to solve this problem.

Social Security: More than half of Americans take Social Security early – only 2 percent of men, and 4 percent of women, defer their income to age 70.[2] That behavior tends to cost retirees as much as a 56 percent difference in income at age 70. With Social Security having an inflation factor, the income discrepancy will grow more during retirement. Advisors who can provide meaningful advice on maximizing income will separate themselves from the pack.

Health Care: Health care is the largest inflationary risk for elderly Americans. The uncertainty around premiums, coverages and providers means that planners must have a conversation about who, how and where will health care be provided during retirement. Knowing this and providing quality advice on health care will become more important as baby boomers grow older.

Housing: In the United States, housing wealth is larger than all of the assets under management for both qualified and nonqualified assets. More importantly, many Americans need to downsize or rightsize their housing plans in retirement. Solutions around the proper use of housing wealth and housing lifestyle will only grow in importance as our clients transition from a working career to retirement.

These are just a few of the demographic and social concerns our industry faces as this generation heads to an unknown retirement. Few, if any, of these concerns are likely to be answered by a computer screen and an algorithm. Instead, these issues are real life concerns that need to be discussed, weighed, informed and addressed with a meaningful and purposeful process. I am confident our profession is well positioned for success for the next several decades.

Winning Strategy: Look at all the demographic and social changes around us today. These changes will influence many of our clients and prospects for several years to come. If you can address these problems, you are likely to gain market share in your business.

[1]LIMRA, *Fact Book on Retirement Income 2016: https://www.limra.com/bookstore/item_details.aspx?sku=23518-001*
[2]*The Motley Fool, "When Does the Average American Start Collecting Social Security?" April 19, 2016: https://www.fool.com/retirement/general/2016/04/19/when-does-the-average-american-start-collecting-so.aspx*

Why Annuity Awareness?

June 1, 2017

These days, it seems there is a holiday for every little occasion. At times, I think because everything is a higher priority moment, nothing seems truly important anymore. The financial service industry is no different, with several months highlighting products throughout the year.

That said, June is Annuity Awareness Month. While I'm biased as an income planning specialist, I think it's important to highlight why annuities are so important to consider with clients.

A recent ThinkAdvisor article highlighted the growing number of people aging to 100:[1]

- In 1900, only 31 people out of 100,000 had reached age 100
- In 1999, that number grew to 1,471
- As of 2010, that number exceeded 1,900, making a 25 percent increase in just the last decade

We have more Americans living longer than ever before but our savings and wealth has not changed significantly to keep pace with the longer life expectancies. We must add guaranteed income to our plans to protect against living longer than expected.

Need More Reasons?

Except for high inflationary times or around the financial crisis, the American savings rate has steadily declined over the past 40 years. The result is a median account balance of $130,100 for trailing baby boomers (age 50-59).[2] This puts our industry in a position where we need to create more income from fewer assets than ever before. Mortality credits associated with annuities can boost yields and incomes to help close the gap.

Due to means testing in health care premiums, longevity concerns have become more critical in client discussions. Tax efficiency in modified adjusted gross income and combined income levels can reduce premiums by 20-30 percent at different tax brackets. Managing the tax burden on income with tax preference products like annuities can be beneficial to clients paying health care premiums to the government.

In addition to general health care, long-term care can't be ignored as a longevity risk. Asset-based long-term care provides the opportunity to take existing tax-deferred annuities and create tax-free distributions when the client needs them most. As planners, we must do a better job of matching the asset with the potential need in the future – not just the funding, but the taxation of the benefits.

Be Aware of Your Practice

Too often, we get stuck in the same sales process and product mix. Use Annuity Awareness Month to look at ways to better leverage annuities with your clients. Take the time to find out how annuities can work in the best interests of a client or prospect. Our economy and demographics are changing, and we need a fresh look at solutions that will make a difference for Americans.

Winning Strategy: In June, look for ways to use annuities in your financial planning practice. Whether you're looking to close an income gap, create more tax efficiency, fund long-term care or just provide more stability, give annuities a chance to prove their value.

[1] *ThinkAdvisor, "Life Expectancy Holds Steady, but Not for 95-Year-Olds," http://www. thinkadvisor.com/2017/04/12/life-expectancy-holds-steady-but-not-for-95-year-o*
[2] *LIMRA, "Fact Book on Retirement Income 2016," https://www.limra.com/bookstore/ item_details.aspx?sku=23518-001*

Why Your Clients Really Care About Guaranteed Income

June 8, 2017

Recently, our division sponsored Wendy Boglioli as a speaker for one of our partner firms. I always enjoy being around Wendy. She is an Olympic champion swimmer, a long-term care advocate and a genuine professional. If you need a great, motivating speaker, I highly encourage you to consider Wendy.

During the event, Wendy spoke about how her swim coaches prepared her team for races. They were ready for anything to go wrong. And, a lot of things can go wrong:

- The starting block might be slippery and you can get off the block awkwardly
- Your goggles can fill up with water
- You can be off a few inches on your turn at the wall
- You can miss a breath due to the waves in the water

The list goes on. The same goes for financial planning; you have to plan for the unexpected.

Personal Case Study

Guaranteed income creates a safety net for many unexpected events and economic conditions. I offer my own parents as an example.

Over the last four decades, my parents have endured several cardiac events. Medical advances since my father's first heart attack have lengthened his life expectancy, but possibly at the risk of the quality of his last years. Guaranteed income sources have allowed them to establish reserve funds for their escalating care need.

I don't think my parents thought my dad would live to age 88 when he retired before the age of 62. Dad's company helped him bridge the gap between his retirement date and early Social Security income. Additionally, both my parents had pension plans to receive regular, guaranteed income. They wrapped their government and pension payments with selected annuity payments from annuities purchased decades ago. Finally, they had a portion invested in equities and bonds to provide growth. But, Dad has received multiples of the cash balance in his pension plan with no care in the world about its rate of return or upside potential.

That's why annuities and guaranteed income are so important to Americans today. The use of mortality credits in annuities provides guaranteed income without concern for rates, market corrections or managing assets.

Through the years, my mom and dad have been able to travel the world, manage their medical expenses and create a healthy standard of living. While their health care is largely an unknown in the future, the reality is that guaranteed income gives them an avenue for stability in a world filled with uncertainty.

Winning Strategy: Take the time to look at how guaranteed income can fit into the portfolio for your next client. We find that 15-25 percent of a portfolio should generate guaranteed income to make it efficient. Talk to your clients about what it will mean to them to be assured they have a consistent income regardless of portfolio performance. I think they will appreciate the value of guaranteed income.

Crossing the Threshold to Fiduciary

June 9, 2017

Implementation is here. The U.S. Department of Labor did not pursue another delay to its fiduciary rule, and the deadline has come to pass. Even though many people in our industry would have preferred more time, I believe now is the right time to refocus our attention on our clients. The fiduciary rule will be a change, but the transitionary period offers relaxed rules to comply.

For the past 14 months, I have been writing about redefining your business. Now that we are crossing the threshold to the rule, my message is the same. This transitionary period offers a chance to continue the thought pattern around how your business should look in 24-36 months.

I have always thought there are two key questions that you need to ask yourself:

- Do you want to move up market?
- Do you want to remain in the same market and become more efficient?

Regardless of the final rule, revisions or revocations, your business will need to look differently than it does today. The marketplace is demanding more holistic planning and a fiduciary mandate. The real question is:

How do you rise above the other fiduciaries
who are born out of regulation?

I think you separate yourself by the way you segment your client base, the services you provide, and frequency of service you provide to your top clients. If you move up market, you will need to really concentrate on segmenting your business and making sure there is a successor to your less than "A" clients. Additionally, you will need to make sure you have the right resources around you in order to compete in the higher net worth marketplace.

According to an American Institute of CPAs/Harris Poll in March 2017, 88 percent of Americans worry about running out of money and having to return to the workforce. If you redefine your business to focus on guaranteed income and longevity issues, I think you will have an opportunity to thrive in a fiduciary world and create differentiation between you and other planners.

The Low Interest Rate Opportunity You're Missing

June 15, 2017

Annuity Awareness Month means different things to different people. Personally, I like to concentrate on the proper uses of annuities, regardless of the economic environment.

Too often, especially lately, I hear advisors talking about rates being too low to consider annuities. But, I think low interest rates provide a unique opportunity to show how annuities create tax efficiencies in income planning.

As planners, one of the obstacles we face is the misuse of social systems for income. Today, only 4 percent of women and 2 percent of men elect to take Social Security at age 70 to gain the maximum income for life on an inflation-adjusted basis.* I talk to many advisors and clients about maximizing the government's programs as a base income level. Single-premium annuities can be a perfect fit for bridging the gap between early retirement and higher income levels for life.

Take a Closer Look

With today's "low interest rate environment," annuities generate a more tax-efficient income than ever before. If you position a single-premium immediate annuity with an eight-year period certain, 95.6 percent of the income is tax free (return of basis). This allows you to position income with nonqualified assets between ages 62 and 70 equal to what would have been early retirement income levels. With tax-free distributions, you can lower the client's tax bracket, allowing you to convert pretax dollars in an individual retirement account to after-tax dollars using Roth conversions.

The net effect is that your client …

- Converts more of their qualified funds at the lowest possible tax bracket
- Maximizes their Social Security benefits
- Gains a higher lifetime income
- Is more likely to receive tax-free distributions after five years from the Roth conversions

All along, the income annuity earns a 1.16 percent rate of return (as of May 2017), which is typically higher than most certificate of deposit rates and comparable to U.S. Treasury rates for similar durations.

So, if you ask your clients if they would like to maximize their Social Security, reduce the tax on their qualified money, and create more lifetime income, how many do you think would say, "Tell me more"? My guess is that will start a conversation with a client or prospect. And, that's why I get excited about making your clients aware of annuities during low interest rate period – tax efficiency.

Winning Strategy: Talk to your clients who have indicated that they want to retire early, at 62 or 65. Give them options that create tax efficiency in their portfolio, regardless of the interest rate environment. Make your clients aware of the possibilities with annuities. That's real #AnnuityAwareness.

The Motley Fool, "When Does the Average American Start Collecting Social Security?" April 19, 2016: https://www.fool.com/retirement/general/2016/04/19/when-does-the-average-american-start-collecting-so.aspx

Why Annuities? Why Now?

June 22, 2017

Annuity Awareness Month allows me to continue talking about why I remain bullish on annuities after the June 9 implementation of the impartial conduct standard. Many advisors said they planned to stop writing annuities after the rule went into effect. I argue that annuities should become a larger part of the product mix for many Americans, especially today.

Close the Gap: A recent Merrill Lynch study indicated that the average American would need more than $700,000 in income for their retirement years.[1] At the same time, LIMRA's 2016 Fact Book reported the median long-term savings in the United States is $130,100.[2] As planners, we will have to make more income with fewer assets than ever before. Using mortality credits to boost the yield in our income vehicles will provide additional income to close the retirement gap.

Don't Wait for Tomorrow's Rates: We live in one of the safest economies in the world. As our world becomes even more unsettled, global investors continue to drive the 10-year Treasury lower as more money flows to the U.S. Treasurys. Too often, I hear people are waiting for the final 2-3 percent of growth in this long bull stock market. The reality is we are a few world events, such as last year's Brexit, from having interest rates near 125-150 bps. Now, not later, is the time to consider protecting our clients' wealth with guaranteed products and income.

Don't Miss Out on Today's Credits: Life expectancies continue to increase, and carriers will be forced to change their mortality crediting tables as more people live longer. Like waiting for interest rates, we are more likely to see a shift downward toward lower payout rates than we have today. The industry will eventually be forced to adapt to the changing demographics in the next 10-15 years. At that time, guaranteed income payouts will likely drop significantly. So, talking to your clients about locking into today's pricing will likely secure higher payouts than waiting for rates or other events.

Turn Savings Into Income: Our society continues to transition to defined contribution plans for convenience and tax-deferred growth. The loss of guaranteed income from employer-sponsored plans will be felt for the next two or three decades as we look to stabilize income planning for near retirees. It's rare that I talk to a plan sponsor who has significant knowledge about converting assets to income. The current working generation has been taught to follow the green line or sit on the orange bench and calculate their asset value. Few retirees know the complexities of retirement income and the proper use of guaranteed incomes.

All of the above create challenges for our industry and clients, but they also offer opportunities for holistic planners to add value to their practice. The fiduciary rule may scare some income planners away from annuities, which will create a void in the marketplace for the planning community to fill. I suggest we take advantage of the situation and add value to our clients' plans.

Winning Strategy: Now is the right time to look at annuities and guaranteed income. Economic conditions and mortality may work against future product pricing, so take the opportunity to lock in today's great environment and bring value to your clients.

[1]Merrill Lynch/Age Wave: "Finances in Retirement: New Challenges, New Solutions," https://mlaem.fs.ml.com/content/dam/ML/Articles/pdf/ML_Finance-Study-Report_2017.pdf
[2]LIMRA, "Fact Book on Retirement Income 2016," https://www.limra.com/bookstore/item_details.aspx?sku=23518-001

Quant-Run Wall Street: Why You Need to Pay Attention

June 29, 2017

At the end of May, I read a Wall Street Journal article about how many quantitative analysts (aka quants) run Wall Street now.* The article focused on bonus payments and regulation around algorithmic-driven trading. It made me think of the impact of the transformations on Wall Street.

The impact of algorithmic-driven trading is swift, steep and game-changing. As an advisor, you'll need to adapt to the way Wall Street trades – even if you remain in the fixed, indexed and income annuity marketplace. Clients should have a balanced portfolio with guaranteed income, equities and bonds. But, equity trading is rapidly changing. With quants driving performance and trading, large blocks of business are likely to change hands quickly going forward.

How does that affect you? A quant-driven Wall Street will likely see wider and steeper movements during corrections. In past corrections, investors have moved to conservative positions when they "see" the first signs of a downward correction. In the future, with algorithms dictating trades, it's entirely possible to get caught in the tsunami of a correction and never "see" the signs like old times.

You need to recognize that the markets are driven more by technology and formulas and less by emotions and human behavior. That means your clients, who still make decisions on emotions and behavior, will likely be left in the dust during market downturns. Your clients are at a disadvantage against a quant.

Winning Strategy: Be proactive. The lack of urgency in our economy troubles me. Talk to your clients about the changes on Wall Street and how they will be affected – secondarily, not just by investments. Create urgency to protect their wealth that has increased over the last eight years, while remaining bullish on equities through an FIA.

Wall Street Journal, "The Quants Run Wall Street Now," May 21, 2017: https://www. wsj.com/articles/the-quants-run-wall-street-now-1495389108

Taking Control of Taxes in Retirement

July 6, 2017

One of the definitions for control is "to hold in check." Another is, "to exercise restraint or direction over." I think both are applicable when it comes to the goals of many retirement investors. No one wants to completely avoid their obligation to support our shared services, i.e., pay their share of taxes. However, everyone I talk to wants to reduce their portion or make sure the tax is used appropriately.

Let me give you an example of control. As I drive to my in-laws' house with my wife, many times during the three-hour drive, our definition of comfortable is different. She tends to set the passenger side of the car much cooler than I like it. In our car, each vent allows the air flow to be reduced or completely shut off. The car's fan continues to push air through, but, when blocked, the air gets pushed out of another vent – on the driver's side. When the temperature gets too warm, the air flow can be opened again on the passenger side. The air flow has changed direction while being held in check on one side of the car. The vent (or, I suppose, my wife) has exercised control.

Pulling the Levers

In retirement, tax control vehicles such as annuities allow investors to decide when and how they pay tax. The flexibility of annuities provides a mechanism to turn income on and off, and choose how to distribute the tax consequences associated with the income. Annuities can also provide a tool to distribute assets to the next generation or second generation, which can provide additional tax control.

Having tax control in your retirement vehicles creates an important lever for income planning. Just like the vents in the car, investors can exercise control over their income and tax consequences. You can elect to turn on income when you need it and decide how much you need. Additionally, the manner in which you accept the cash flow dictates how you pay tax. Distributions may be taxed as gain first or with an exclusion ratio. You may want to tax your distributions as gain first if you are in a lower tax bracket when you begin income. Otherwise, you may want to spread the tax consequences over the rest of your life. What's important is that an annuity gives you choice and control.

Looking at More Options

The stretch IRA (individual retirement arrangement) provision is now being challenged in Congress, and IRA holders may only be able to stretch $450,000 to the next generation. Nonqualified annuities allow for multiple distribution options that include skipping generations. The beneficiary designations of annuities provide greater flexibility and control versus institutional IRAs. While those designations add no value in the accumulation phase, the tax control at death and during the income phase can add several basis points to the overall return of the annuity. There is additional value to tax control vehicles beyond the simple interest rate.

Between "holding in check" and "exercising restraint and direction over," controlling taxes remains an important part of the retirement income discussion. Make sure you have the appropriate control over income and taxes as you plan your clients' strategies. Tax laws change often – in fact, there were 31 changes in U.S. tax rates in the 34 years between 1979 and 2013.* So it's important to create flexibility and control in the financial plan.

Winning Strategy: Have tax control embedded in your financial plans. Choosing when and how you pay tax is an important discussion point for clients looking to retire. Tax deferral is important during the accumulation phase, but it can also add basis points to your income and distribution strategy at death.

*Tax Policy Center, Statistics: http://www.taxpolicycenter.org/statistics/historical-average-federal-tax-rates-all-household

Why Now is the Time to Talk About Pension Risk Transfers

June 13, 2017

When it comes to corporate decisions, tax considerations are always in play. Given the current and potential tax laws, now is a good time to talk to your corporate clients about taking their pension obligations off the table. Aside from the tax impact, there are several good reasons to have the conversation with your clients.

Pension plans continue to lose their status in retirement planning for a lot of small to midsize corporations. While defined benefit plans can make sense for a lot of single-employer plans, they largely do not help recruit talent for many businesses in America. Small pension contributions don't seem to entice younger workers or recent college graduates as much as profit sharing or stock option incentives. That's because the value of guaranteed income is lost on many of workers younger than 45 years old.

The cost of administering a defined plan continues to escalate as well. Even for fully funded plans, the cost of Pension Benefit Guaranty Corporation (PBGC) premiums will increase 25 percent by 2019.[1] So, even if your corporate client makes no changes in their plan, it will cost more to simply have the plan – even if it is not being offered to new employees.

One solution could be a Pension Risk Transfer (PRT). A PRT gives a corporation multiple benefits:

- Transfers the risk of longevity from the plan to an insurer
- Eliminates future administration and shifts the service to a third party
- Frees up existing corporate resources dedicated to the plan
- Provides a potential current deduction to make plan assets whole
- Guarantees the commitment made to employees is honored, without leveraging company cash flow

By transferring plan assets to an insurer, the corporation shifts many of its pension obligation risks. And, as many believe that tax reform might happen in the next 18-24 months, corporate assets can be used to bring plan obligations to 100 percent funding levels. In doing so, those contributions receive a tax deduction in today's higher corporate tax brackets.

For too long, corporations have ignored their defined benefit plan obligations. Now, we find that many employers have underfunded plans, which puts many retirees' guaranteed income plans at risk. With today's tax rates, it's a prime time to engage corporate clients in using stale and underperforming assets to complete the obligations that were made to so many current and past employees.

Honor the Intent

When talking about pensions, it is rarely about interest rates or performance of the plan assets. Without a doubt, the valuation of the assets comes into play. In reality, executives want to honor the commitment they made to the employees who helped build the company. For decades, pensions have been the way to reward employees. Now, it's time to make sure that actually happens.

Tax rates, interest rate risk, and longevity risks all play into managing pension assets. Our tax policy favors contributing to plan assets now. There is considerable uncertainty in the world today, and the potential rise or fall of interest rates will affect bond values. Bonds continue to make up large portions of corporate pension plans, so our retirees are truly at risk.

Even with plans that are wholly funded, the assumptions from two decades ago do not account for today's longer life expectancies. We increase our life span by 2.5 years for every decade in America.[2] Therefore, with a normal, 20-year retirement, pension plans really need to have 25 percent more assets than they do today. It's time to pay attention to this retirement risk and make it an opportunity to help corporations meet the obligations they promised.

Winning Strategy: Even with a fully funded pension plan, increased longevity has likely not been accounted for. With changes in tax policy and asset performance, transferring pension risk from a corporate balance sheet to an insurer makes perfect sense today. Take the chance to talk with employers about how they can benefit from PRT.

[1]*Society for Human Resource Management, "Study: Pension Plans Overpay PBGC Premiums by Millions," April 12, 2017: https://www.shrm.org/resourcesandtools/hr-topics/benefits/pages/pensions-overpay-pbgc-premiums.aspx*
[2]*Population Health Metrics, "Changes in Life Expectancy 1950–2010: Contributions from Age- and Disease-Specific Mortality in Selected Countries," 2016: https://www.ncbi.nlm.nih.gov/pmc/articles/PMC4877984/*

The 4 Key Advantages of HECMs in Income Planning

July 20, 2017

I spend a lot of time on the road. Not just for my job, but also because my wife and I both have families who live within four hours driving distance of our house. Making sure everyone's favorite Uncle Mike makes it to the latest family event requires some flexibility. On many of those long drives through Indiana, I have found the GPS route that delivers me to my destination changes from one day to the next. Because of traffic, weather or construction, I end up taking alternate routes on roads I'm not familiar with. But sometimes the alternate route is best.

Helping clients navigate the ever-changing retirement income market means you have to be innovative. Maybe you've never heard of using Home Equity Conversion Mortgages (HECMs) as part of an income planning strategy. Regardless, it's time to talk to clients about this alternative vehicle.

There are unique advantages to using housing wealth as part of the income planning process. This tool does not work in every situation, but it can provide added income and flexibility for many clients. Here are some key advantages:

1. **Income from HECMs is received tax-free.** I talk a lot about the importance of what you keep versus what you earn. The use of tax-free income can be beneficial in many ways. First, it reduces combined income for Social Security taxation, which

can provide relief for many middle class Americans. With means testing on Medicare, a slight reduction under a tax threshold can create as much as a $1,800 difference in medical premiums. Paying attention to client incomes and potential thresholds will become an important planning criteria as health care becomes more difficult to predict.

2. **HECM lines of credit grow annually.** If set up properly, a HECM credit line grows between 4 percent and 6 percent annually in current interest rate environments. If you qualify for a $200,000 credit line at age 62, it will grow to more than $525,000 at age 82. That pool of money is available for any purpose, at any time, with no taxation, regardless of the value of the home. Because the newer HECM products are nonrecourse loans, the client does not risk losing their home if the local real estate market doesn't grow accordingly.

3. **The flexibility of HECMS provides options for many near-retirees and retirees.** Once established, the HECM doesn't need to be revalued. It's there for as long as the client lives in the home. A financial literacy quiz showed that only one in four Americans had thought about how their Social Security benefits may be reduced after the death of a spouse.* Housing wealth can give the surviving spouse access to income without having to manage the funds like a traditional investment.

4. **HECM for Purchase strategies can allow retirees to move to a more appropriate home without increasing their mortgage payments.** One of the most neglected client conversations is the discussion around where they will live in retirement. With longevity increasing, many of our clients will not want to live in the same multistory home where they raised their children. At the same time, they are not willing to add more expense to an already compressed income after their working years. So, a HECM for Purchase allows a new home to be purchased without a traditional amortization schedule.

As our clients age and navigate multiple longevity-related issues, it's important to maintain flexibility in their plans. HECMs can provide liquidity when they need it most. And, these tools can take pressure off existing assets under management during the income distribution phase.

Winning Strategy: There's more than one path to a successful retirement plan. Look at alternatives to relieve pressure from assets under management – tools like HECMs can provide flexibility and put your clients in suitable housing. You can help your clients be in the driver's seat as they retire and face longevity risks.

*The American College RICP® Retirement Income Literacy Survey, September 2014, p. 88: http://retirement.theamericancollege.edu/sites/retirement/files/Retirement_Income_Literacy_Survey_Full_Report_0.pdf

Take Advantages of Today's Tax Laws
July 27, 2017

Looks can be deceiving. Nowhere is that truer than in retirement planning. The client who drives a modest car, wears jeans and eats at Bob Evans ends up being the millionaire next door, while the flashy dresser with the fancy watch has a pile of debt and little to no nest egg to fall back on.

Looks can also be deceiving when it comes to investments. All too often, clients get caught up in seeking the highest rate of return they can find in an investment. Unfortunately, many don't always walk away with the best net return because of what's hidden underneath: taxes and fees.

Just like a fancy watch, those attractive, high interest rates do not tell the whole story. Within many typical, non-annuity-type investments, there are certain pieces of drag embedded in the total return.

- There are sales charges with the purchase or redemption of the asset
- There may be annual fees for overall investment and planning

- Perhaps the most harmful are capital gains and ordinary income taxes – those can cost clients more than a third of return on an annual basis

So the initial high interest rate that enticed the client ends up being irrelevant after taxes and charges eat into it.

Don't Miss Out by Misunderstanding

Like I said, sometimes you will find the modest, jeans-wearing client ends up having the highest net worth. In the same vein, annuities are plain and simple but offer surprisingly essential benefits. One of the strongest reasons to position part of a portfolio with annuities is to take advantage of the tax-deferred growth. During the accumulation phase, the asset grows without the drag of either capital gain or ordinary income tax.

Now, some will argue that the deferral creates a larger tax bill at distribution. But, that's only true if you completely liquidate the annuity. If the goal is to live off the annuity with just interest and systematic withdrawals during retirement, you will have created a much larger nest egg during accumulation rather than paying taxes annually. After all, "It's not what you earn – it's what you keep," and annuities are instrumental in helping the client keep more.

Build a Bridge

Additionally, the low interest rate and favorable tax treatment of annuities creates a unique planning opportunity to help maximize Social Security benefits. By bridging early income at age 62 with a nonqualified, single-premium immediate annuity (SPIA) rather than starting Social Security, as much as 96 percent of the client's income is tax-free. This bridge allows the client to minimize tax drag on their income and wait to maximize their Social Security benefits at age 70.

The difference in Social Security income at age 62 versus age 70 might be as high as a 50 percent. That increase might translate to more travel, more time with family, or a larger cushion for necessities like medication. More importantly, this strategy affords the client to have more of their money linked to income that keeps pace with inflation, and inflation might be the cruelest tax of all.

Today, the average younger baby boomer (aged 50-59) has only saved $130,100, so it's critical to create as much asset value as possible in the future.[1] Tax laws are always changing – in fact, there were 31 changes in U.S. tax rates in the 34 years between 1979 and 2013.[2] So you have to take advantage of what's available now. It's important to help your clients remove their "interest rate blinders" and see the many benefits of annuities – benefits they might miss on first glance.

Winning Strategy: Many people do not realize the powerful tax advantages of annuities. Plan how you can help your clients seize the opportunity of the current tax laws governing annuities. The disparity between annuities and other investments may not last long.

[1]LIMRA, "Fact Book on Retirement Income 2016": https://www.limra.com/bookstore/item_details.aspx?sku=23518-001
[2]Tax Policy Center, Statistics: http://www.taxpolicycenter.org/statistics/historical-average-federal-tax-rates-all-household

How to Flip Your Strategy from Accumulation to Income

August 3, 2017

Winning sometimes requires looking at alternatives. That doesn't mean you win with illegal actions or without integrity. Instead, it means attacking a challenge differently than you normally would. You do so because your opponent is unique and the consequences of losing are high.

On the Offense

In 1984, I had the privilege of seeing one of the greatest minds in basketball, Coach Bob Knight, prepare for a regional semifinal game against the No. 1 team in the country and the defending national champions. The opponent, the University of North Carolina, played with a half-court trapping defense that had been a staple of their legendary coach, Dean Smith. Their team consisted of players that many college basketball fans recognize: Brad Daugherty, Matt Doherty,

Sam Perkins and a guard by the name of Michael Jordan. (He was as great a player in college as he was in the NBA.)

Losing this game would mean Indiana's season would come to an end and there would be no chance at a regional or national title. So, we had to look at this mighty opponent differently in order to have success.

As a student manager, during the week of preparation, I took several messages to Coach Knight. He sought out advice from basketball icons like Henry Iba and Pete Newell. We played a motion offense and typically had our guards bring the ball up the court. We started four freshmen that year and, with Carolina's press so disruptive, our young team might have folded under the pressure. So, we needed to look at alternatives.

Coach Knight practiced with our guards positioned in the corner so we had an outlet to relieve ourselves of the pressure. Additionally, we experimented with having our big men bring the ball up the court while having our smaller guards in the low post. Essentially, we flipped the court on the opposing team and took our biggest risk – their half-court trapping defense – off the table.

An Alternate Defense

In retirement, our clients face several risks, and the consequences are just as devastating – you don't get a second chance at planning retirement. Therefore, you need to take risks off the table by thinking alternatively. Today's economic environment presents several ways to look at alternatives to improve retirement.

- We have historically low interest rates, making it more difficult to retire through capital preservation
- Most people believe that over the next three to five years we will see increasing interest rates that might depreciate the bond values that many look to for safety
- Our government continues to manipulate monetary policy, making it uncertain how bond markets will react to "uncensored" interest rate movements
- We continue to be part of an extended bull run following the financial crisis that many believe is running out of steam

It's more important than ever to look at alternatives, especially for those invested in bonds. Fixed indexed annuities can provide alternative income streams, protection from markets risks and tax deferral. I encourage everyone to look at alternatives and share them with your clients.

Winning Strategy: Retirement is the most complex problem your clients will ask you to solve. You can't win the game with the same strategy you used during accumulation. Instead, you have to consider alternatives to better your clients' probability of success during retirement.

Why Product Allocation Matters More than Asset Allocation

August 10, 2017

Several years ago, I attended a continuing education seminar from an insurance carrier. And recently, one of my co-workers gave a webinar about tax efficiency using life insurance. Both reminded me of how quickly we drift back to old habits of asset allocation.

So, I went through my continuing education files and found the case study from the seminar several years ago. Surprisingly, even with the drop in interest rates, the example still provides value to many retirees and their portfolios. Let me share it with you.

The Situation

A husband and wife are both age 65 and getting ready to retire. Like many Americans, they have no pension plan but have managed to create a nest egg of $750,000. They have $20,000 of Social Security income between the two of them, starting at age 65. The difference in income, $30,000, needs to come from the assets under management using a systematic withdrawal strategy. That withdrawal equates to a 4 percent distribution.

You may be thinking this sounds like a lot of your middle class American clients. And, you would be right. As I travel around the country, I see a lot of clients taking income off their assets through a more conservative asset allocation. But here are the problems with this setup:

- There is no guaranteed income for life outside of Social Security
- Research indicates that the 4 percent withdrawal rate may be too aggressive, regardless of asset allocation modeling
- 60 percent of their income would stop if they run out of money, which puts pressure on the management of the assets and the allocation strategy
- Essentially, the clients may be forced to take on more risk (assume more return) later in life when volatility might not be appropriate

The Solution

Now, let's look alternatively at product allocation and how beneficial it can be to our sample client. The client places $100,000 in a fixed indexed annuity with a guaranteed income rider that generates $5,000 annually. Next, they purchase a $160,000 single-premium income annuity that pays $9,000 per year. Both are guaranteed for both the lives of the husband and wife, no matter how long they live. Finally, $490,000 remains in the asset allocation strategy, where they take $16,000 of annual income from the account.

Here are the improvements with this strategy that generates the same $30,000 of income:

- $34,000, or 68 percent, of the total income will never stop, regardless of how long they live, even if they run out of money in their assets under management; Social Security may adjust after the first death, but income will continue
- Only $16,000 of their income is at risk if their account balance draws down to zero
- The systematic withdrawal is now just 3.3 percent; it's still not at the recommended 2.85 percent, but it is less than the 4 percent strategy before the product allocation

The Takeaway

Product allocation is more important than asset allocation. The use of guaranteed income can provide the leverage needed to lower withdrawal rates and increase the stability ratio of the entire income portfolio.

Winning Strategy: Product allocation should be the first thing you look at when constructing an income portfolio. Think about the location of products and income assets before assigning an asset allocation strategy.

Part III
In a Post-DOL World

We've Already Passed the Finish Line:
A DOL Comment

August 10, 2017

Today (Aug. 10, 2017), the U.S. Department of Labor's request to delay the fiduciary rule's full implementation was revealed. As with most regulation, there are technical aspects to the delay that will likely be argued by supporters and opponents. I want to make one thing clear: We've already passed the finish line for fiduciary status.

Undoubtedly, the rule's documentation could be less onerous. But, we shouldn't ignore the fact that fiduciary status is here – and it's here to stay. We must adapt to it. We must innovate toward it. We must improve our client experience. We must keep our clients' interests before our own. And, we must move the retirement income community forward … now.

Many people will use this announcement to recommend going back to the old ways of doing business. It's too late. Clients are beginning to ask their financial advisors if they are fiduciaries. Working with the clients' interests has always been a priority, and the way that we operate our business.

Today – really since the release of the proposal in 2016 – fiduciary status is a table stake, a requirement and, most importantly, an expectation. In order to be successful in business, you have to meet or exceed the clients' expectations. The value you bring is determined by how much you bring to the client above what they paid. The client expects maximum value, so you have to look at your marketplace beyond the regulation.

The market has already begun to shift toward working in fiduciary status for all client relationships. Transparency continues to grow as an integral part of pricing fees and commissions. Disclosure has become a part of the product fulfillment process. Greater client awareness and education about solutions have become part of more sales presentations. In many ways, our industry has improved more in the last 12 months than it has in the last decade.

I encourage those in the retirement income space to continue the move forward toward the fiduciary world. That doesn't mean some of the DOL's unintended consequences don't need to be dealt with over the next 18 months. And, moving toward a fiduciary world doesn't mean the elimination of commissions. However, we can't go back on our commitment to serve our clients. With the complexity of retirement, there has never been a more important time to engage with Americans and help them solve their most difficult problems – longevity and income.

Please stay connected with Ash Brokerage to learn more ideas on how to best serve your clients in an uncertain regulatory and economic environment. Ash has been active in the comment periods, and we look forward to answering our industry challenges through innovation, education and practice enhancement.

Winning Strategy: When you run a race, you never look back. As you change your retirement income practice toward a fiduciary status, don't look back. Keep your focus forward on improving your clients' position, their experience with your firm and how to best serve them.

Low Maintenance Lawns and Portfolios
August 17, 2017

I am not a handyman. Before marrying my wife two years ago, I made it clear she shouldn't expect a lot of home improvement projects from me. Despite knowing that, we bought a 1920s home together.

Now, the home was already fully remodeled. And, I don't regret the decision because we invested in our community and chose to remain a part of downtown Fort Wayne. But, there are still a lot of things to do to "make it our own."

The backyard is a good example. After losing the grass to last summer's heat, we decided to redesign the small backyard. For perspective's sake, it takes me 300 steps to completely mow my front and back yards. That aspect of urban living is great! But, we still had to do something with the yard to make it look decent.

After consulting with a landscaper, we agreed to add a fire pit and some plants. Because we wanted the least amount of maintenance, we choose perennials. By the time we were finished, the landscaper was able to fill the entire space with perennials and mulch, which eliminated the need for any future lawn mowing. This was not my original vision for the space … but I now sit on the back deck and enjoy the backyard.

Low Maintenance Planning

The investment in our new backyard gives me peace of mind because I no longer have to worry about cutting the grass. As I was out on the back deck this week, I thought about the ways alternative investments give peace of mind to so many clients.

- First, annuities can produce guaranteed income that stabilizes the portfolio. Our studies at Ash Brokerage show the impact of guaranteed income can be substantial. I encourage you to look at our white papers and interactive tools that show how much guaranteed income impacts a retiree's income.

- Second, annuities provide market risk protection. In today's uncertain economic climate, clients will likely appreciate the stability that alternative investments can bring. Whether fixed or indexed annuities, these vehicles protect clients from a likely rising interest rate environment.

- Finally, having certainty in the income stream provides peace of mind to many clients, knowing they won't outlive their income.

Look at your client portfolios, especially those that have a bond portion. For clients who are near retirement or in retirement, it makes sense to talk about how annuities can provide stability, security and guaranteed income. Just like I enjoy my low maintenance backyard, your clients will enjoy a low maintenance retirement plan.

Winning Strategy: Peace of mind is an important and immeasurable aspect of retirement planning. Look at alternative investments that can provide stability, security and guaranteed income. Not having to worry about income will make your clients' retirement more enjoyable.

Bond Risks in Retirement

August 24, 2017

We frequently talk about sequence of return risk for a retiree's portfolio. For many people, that risk is associated with equities only; however, bonds carry market risks as well.

Unfortunately, many Americans have looked at bonds as a safe vehicle since the financial crisis. Since that time, interest rates have generally fallen, making bonds an upward trend in prices. Bonds can fit into many portfolios, but we need to consider the risks in today's economic environment. Three things to consider:

1. **Interest rates are at near all-time lows.** When interest rates rise, bond prices decline – rates and bond prices move in opposite directions. Many planners have increased durations in their portfolios to provide more yield to their clients. However, the additional duration poses additional interest rate risk. For example, a five-year bond will have a 4.6 percent decline in value for a 1 percent increase in interest rates. The changes in bond prices are steeper the longer the duration. A 10-year duration bond would have an 8.7 percent drop in value due to the same 1 percent rise in interest rate. Given where we are on all segments of the yield curve, it's likely to see rate increases over the next three to five years. This potentially creates sequencing risk on what many investors believe to be safety.

2. **Coupon rates continue to be low.** I would argue that they are artificially low due to the financial crisis and the struggling economy. Regardless, it takes more than two times the capital to generate the same income than it did pre-financial crisis. For example, you could find a 5 percent coupon in 2009-10. It would only take $400,000 of capital to generate $20,000 of income. Today, it would take $815,000 to recreate the $20,000 of annual income. Notwithstanding a reversal of current monetary policy, these rates are likely to rise but very slowly. So, retirees don't benefit from waiting.

3. **Bonds can certainly be sold quickly in today's markets.** By definition, that makes the instrument highly liquid. In reality, bonds may be sold at a substantial loss as described above. Depending on performance, bonds can be illiquid due to market conditions, and you can't dictate when an emergency requires liquidation of capital for specific purposes.

So, how do annuities stack up to the risks of bond portfolios?

Regardless of fixed or indexed, annuities provide no downside market risks. While fixed annuities may limit the growth potential, they protect the downside, making them more appropriate than ever to position into the portfolio.

Income generation can be just as healthy using income riders versus relying on the coupon rate of the bond. In today's marketplace, the client can easily find 4.5-5 percent distribution rates on capital. This means you would only need $400,000-$445,000 in order to generate the same $20,000.

While most annuities have surrender charges due to their market protection and general account status, most products provide liquidity each year up to a certain percentage and for critical illnesses. In many cases, the surrender charge can be less than the loss of a bond value change, especially for longer durations.

A bond portfolio provides diversity opposite an equity asset. And, bonds can be extremely useful as a part of the asset allocation strategy to maximize the efficient frontier. A mix of bonds and equities lessens the volatility while increasing the return. However, we need to consider alternatives to bonds in the current rate and economic conditions. There is as much risk in bonds as there is in the equity market in the current climate.

Winning Strategy: Look at your bond holdings. If those clients are getting ready to turn those bonds into income, you might consider the advantages of annuities. The rules change when you turn accumulation into income. When the rules change, you need to change your strategy.

The Immeasurable Return on Family Values

August 31, 2017

While we've had our eyes on the U.S. Department of Labor's fiduciary and conflicts of interest rule, Congress has recommended some new tax laws that might adversely affect the American consumer even more so.

A proposed bill would limit the amount of retirement funds that might be stretched to the next generation or the following generation. The proposal limits the amount a retirement investor can stretch to only $250,000.

This is where you should look at different angles and new ways to attack the problem. Many annuities allow for joint, nonspousal annuitants. The advantage of this setup is that both annuitants get income for both their lives. This allows annuities to be a vehicle that creates a "stretch-like" provision above the $250,000 of assets under management.

More than Money

How would your clients and beneficiaries react to being able to do the following?

- Grandparent receives income on an asset for the rest of their life – guaranteed – with a cost of living increase each year
- When the grandparent passes away, the grandchild receives the same income – guaranteed for their life – with a cost of

living increase each year

- On the grandchild's 16th birthday, the planning firm sends a check plus a note from the grandparent about how special the "Sweet 16" is and to enjoy their teen years
- On the grandchild's 21st birthday, the planning firm sends a larger check plus a note from the grandparent about how important family values are as an adult – the grandparent writes about the fears they had when they were 21 and how they succeeded
- When the grandchild weds, the newlyweds get a letter from the grandparent about the secrets to a 50-year marriage, and reaffirms the family values that helped them weather the storms
- When the couple have their first child, a letter arrives talking about how challenging parenting will be, but the rewards of raising a child far outweigh the early mornings, teething, potty-training, and other heartaches in raising a child. The letter reassures them everyone has been there and, if they stick to the family values, their child will be successful, healthy and wealthy.
- And so on … and so on …

In these cases, the return on money becomes irrelevant. You are not helping your clients pass along just tax savings or a better return; you are perpetuating value that is important – their family values.

Winning Strategy: Talk to your clients who have grandchildren. Show them how they could create a stretch provision that is not dictated by tax law. Instead, it is driven by their family values – I think they will find the idea more valuable than any return you could provide. And, it will likely give the family even more than you can ever provide through asset allocation.

3 Ways to Use Life Insurance in Retirement Plans

September 7, 2017

September is Life Insurance Awareness Month. Why should this matter to you? Because the percentage of households that own life insurance continues to fall. We have recently changed the face of "financial planning" to only engage with clients through asset management services. Worse yet, our industry refers to that engagement as "wealth management."

The idea of wealth management should dictate holistic planning, which includes basis risk management, income stability during retirement, legacy goals, tax planning and health care planning – both medical and long-term care. However, our industry falls short of holistic planning. The first step is to look how our asset managers and retirement advisors can benefit from a healthy and robust annuity partnership. Below are three quick ideas to bridge the gap for our clients.

1. We find that many of our clients don't need to live off their required minimum distributions (RMDs) in retirement. Currently, some clients elect to defer their RMDs using a qualified longevity annuity contract (QLAC). Instead, we need to evaluate whether our clients would rather transfer more wealth via life insurance. By using the RMDs to purchase life insurance, they can pass more qualified funds to the next generation, and the transition happens tax-free instead of at the highest tax bracket.

2. Our research shows that the use of a noncorrelated asset benefits the distribution strategy of most retirees. With any systematic withdrawal strategy, taking the income from a noncorrelated asset improves the success ratio of the income over 20 years. Using multiple iterations, we found that a typical withdrawal strategy fails 23 percent of the time. When we introduce a noncorrelated asset and take withdrawals from it after every down-market year, the strategy fails only 2 percent

of the time. Portfolio values ranged from neutral to as high as $600,000 more in assets under management after 20 years. Noncorrelated assets can be cash, fixed annuities and fixed indexed annuities; however, life insurance and Home Equity Conversion Mortgages (HECMs) provide tax-free access to capital with little or no cost and with flexibility to choose when to initiate the income replacement.

3. The other way to leverage annuities in the planning process is to maximize the long-term care pool of assets and income. There are several ways to accomplish this goal. First, existing annuities may be annuitized for a 10-year period certain (assuming older than age 59 ½) and used to purchase life insurance with new long-term care riders. Second, several carriers have annuity-based long-term care policies. This allows you to take tax deferral that was purchased for emergency purposes and make those gains tax-free for qualified long-term care expenses.

There are many ways annuity producers, financial planners, wealth managers – whatever retirement income planners want to call themselves – can utilize life insurance to better their clients' plans. These are just a few. We will explore some other ideas in September for Life Insurance Awareness Month.

Winning Strategy: For retirement income planners, life insurance should be an integral part of the holistic planning process. Without risk management, income and retirement cash flow can be jeopardized due to unplanned circumstances.

Creating True Liquidity

September 14, 2017

As I travel and speak with different groups and advisors, I'm pleasantly surprised by their willingness to learn how annuities and life insurance can create true and free liquidity. Too often, clients and their advisors view mutual funds, stocks and bonds as the only source of liquidity in the markets.

I agree those instruments provide liquidity due to the markets on which they are listed. However, market risks and sequencing risks may hinder liquidity when you need to convert the vehicle to cash quickly. And, that is the most worthwhile definition of liquidity – the ability to convert something to cash quickly.

If properly used, life insurance and annuities can help create liquidity as part of an overall asset allocation strategy in just about any portfolio. Let me give you a couple of examples.

1. Annuities and life insurance may work as noncorrelated assets in the income phase of retirement. In our studies, we ran 50 simulations using the past 20 years of market sequences. For every year with negative market returns, we took the required income from a noncorrelated asset. Over 20 years, the use of a noncorrelated asset fell from 26 percent to 2 percent. Noncorrelated assets may be found in the form of cash, cash value life insurance, and fixed annuities. The net difference in values was neutral (both had at least one failure) to as much as $621,000 in portfolio value. This can create overall liquidity when you don't want to liquidate securities during bear markets.

2. Our research also shows that most retirees can maximize their income and create the most liquidity with 15-25 percent of the portfolio producing guaranteed income. Guaranteed income comes from three sources: Social Security, defined benefit plans and insurance companies in the form of annuities. With guaranteed income securely positioned, the assets under management are not required to create the retirement income. Those incomes are also more stable due to the fact that the withdrawal percentage is below 4 percent in many instances. This positioning creates a "pool" of assets that are not needed for income purposes. It can be used for charitable purposes, to address health care and long-term care, or maintain a healthy reserve pool for emergencies.

Longevity creates many concerns for retirees. One of the most costly is long-term care. It is an unknown risk and increasing cost in any retirement plan. Today, it is not a capital issue, but rather a cash flow issue. For a client who has a 95 percent probability of success in their retirement plan, their chances of not running out of money with just one, three-year long-term care event reduces their probability of success to 2 percent. Had the client purchased long-term care insurance – either hybrid on a life policy or annuity, or a rider on a life policy – the probability of success is buoyed at 85 percent.

I'm happy to show you these numbers and studies in action, so you can see the impact for yourself. But, the bottom line is this: While the specific product may not create immediate liquidity, annuities and life insurance can provide unrestricted liquidity for many portfolios. The proper use of annuities and life insurance may create many tax advantages by investing in a different asset allocation focused on long-term capital gains. (Please consult a tax advisor for specific benefits.) Take the time to learn how a small portion of the product allocation makes exponential gains in the performance of the income plan.

Winning Strategy: Many times, clients want to do a lot with little money. They end up choosing which priority to address. Look at annuities and life insurance as an alternative. They create liquidity within the portfolio if used properly.

Alternatives for the Uninsured and Underinsured

September 21, 2017

Ownership of life insurance remains at all-time lows. With a few exceptions, it has continued to decline over the last couple of generations. This has left a lot of Americans without life insurance by choice. However, a subset of those people is truly uninsured. They may have never qualified or, like many Americans, they waited until a health concern bubbled up, which made the coverage unaffordable.

Too often, I see planners tell their clients they will have to "self-insure" their future. That translates to becoming more aggressive in their allocation to grow their funds faster. And, keeping more assets in brokerage accounts and wrap accounts instead of shifting their risk. In reality, there are other ways to shift this risk.

Coverage with Leverage

As I've mentioned before, long-term care is more of a cash flow issue than an asset issue. I hear many planners looking to protect assets instead of creating additional cash flow to pay for the care. Annuities can provide a guaranteed income, and many riders accelerate the payment for those confined to a facility or needing home health care. In some cases, the income doubles during the time of need.

Asset-based long-term care products have become a popular solution because clients can maintain control over their account and balance sheet. These products shift the account value to a leveraged situation. You have to ask yourself ...

Who wouldn't want to receive two to three times the value?

To make this solution even more attractive, tax advantages exist due to the Pension Protection Act. Now, some underwriting exists, but this solution offers the best use of a deductible – your account value – followed by the leverage provided by an insurance company.

Many life insurance companies offer enhanced riders that provide part of the death benefit if you qualify for two of the six activities of daily living (ADL). In many cases, these companies underwrite toward the mortality risk and not so much morbidity risk. Again, underwriting exists, but it can help the underinsured capture more risk mitigation.

We have to look at alternatives for our underinsured and uninsurable clients. Simply keeping assets under management presents a conflict of interest by not looking at other risk mitigation tools in the planning process. Take time to serve your clients and evaluate how life insurance and annuities can fit into the income distribution planning strategy.

Winning Strategy: Look at your clients who can't afford traditional insurance coverage or can't qualify for the coverage they want. Alternatives exist where the risk of long-term care can be shifted, in part, to an insurer instead of remaining with the assets under management.

How to Reduce or Eliminate Taxes on Wealth Transfer

September 28, 2017

When estate planners talk about annuities and individual retirement account (IRAs), they say those vehicles are the worst to be holding when you pass away. I generally agree with the statement. Moreover, planners focus on the estate tax and reducing its impact. The deferred gains in a tax-deferred product – qualified or nonqualified – have the tendency to force the gain to be taxed at the recipient's highest marginal tax bracket.

Because those assets become taxed at the highest marginal bracket, it's important to have plans for the tax deferral or qualified accounts in a client's estate. Many planners should look to life insurance as a way to create the necessary capital to pay for the tax. Life insurance also provides the liquidity needed to pay the tax without invading the IRA.

Other planners look to leverage the power of the stretch IRA to minimize taxes and reduce the burden of the overall tax on the beneficiaries. Unfortunately, it appears that Congress is making plans to limit the amount that can be stretched to $250,000. For the mass affluent and middle-America clientele, the loss of the stretch provision might be devastating to wealth transfer.

One Product, Two Tax Strategies

So, how can life insurance work in conjunction with IRAs and tax-deferred vehicles like nonqualified annuities?

1. Life insurance can be used to pay for the income tax on the transfer of wealth. Income tax brackets remain extremely high – as high as 39.6 percent on a federal rate. That doesn't even take into consideration the state tax revenue, which can push it well over 40 percent of the gain being taxed. As I travel

around the country, I don't hear enough people talking about the income tax effect on wealth transfer. Clients and planners hide behind the exemption of the federal or state estate taxes. Unfortunately, those do not apply to income taxes. Creating liquidity to meet the demands of the income tax due the April after the death of the IRA is a smart option. Life insurance pays for the cost of the tax on discounted dollars, and it generates the cash position when people need it most.

2. Qualified assets above those that can be stretched can be transferred to life insurance. This allows the client to turn the transfer of wealth from tax-deferred to tax-free. This can be meaningful to beneficiaries and easier to transfer outside of the estate with proper use of trusts.

Look at your tax-deferred vehicles and identify clients who will pass along not only a big inheritance, but also a big tax bill. Talk to them about using life insurance to reduce overall costs or completely eliminate the federal income tax on transfers of wealth.

Winning Strategy: Life insurance can be meaningful for those with larger IRAs or accounts with tax-deferred gains. These vehicles are the worst to have in your estate on the date of death. There are strategies to reduce or eliminate the income tax.

Why You Must Prepare to Win in 2018

October 5, 2017

It's hard to believe we are already in the fourth quarter of 2017. It may seem like you're still trying to wrap your arms around this year, but it's already time to look at your plans for 2018. Your first step should be to create goals and direction for your practice. We have a full 90 days to prepare for 2018, so there's no excuse for not having a great year.

Being around Coach Bob Knight for four years taught me a lot about planning for success. Many said that if you gave Coach Knight a week to prepare for a team, he would likely win the game. I encourage you to consider the things that he did to plan and apply them to your business.

Set reasonable but high goals for the season. As an owner of your financial services business, you need to have overarching goals for the year. Where do you want your business to be at the end of 2018, and how does that fit into your long-term strategy?

At Indiana University, we had three goals for the season:

- Go undefeated in the pre-conference season
- Win the conference
- Go as far as we could in the NCAA tournament

Each step built on the next. No goal was unreasonable. And, if successful, would add to the history of Indiana basketball and gave our fans great enjoyment. Notice that our goals were to win every game. Conference season is difficult, but it was not unreasonable to think that we could win the conference. We didn't set out to win the NCAA tournament every year, but we wanted to survive and advance as far as our team possibly could.

Assess your strengths and weaknesses – honestly. Coach Knight would consult with many of his mentors to ask how to use certain players. Some players were not good handling the ball; others were lightning quick. Using the players to their strengths was critical to game day and the season's goal attainment.

You need to take a hard look at your personnel and their strengths and weaknesses, even if you are a sole practitioner. My business coach helps me conduct a 360-degree review of both my direct reports and direct superiors. It's uncomfortable to hear confidential and anonymous feedback, but it helps me adjust my leadership of the team – where I need to improve or what they like from me.

You might ask yourself some questions like:

- What do I need to improve in order to hit my 2018 goal?
- How do I need to reshape my products or services in order to grow my business to my goal?
- Are my support and sales staff the right people with the right skill sets to take me to the next level?
- How do I need to reinvest in my people to ensure that I reach

my goals in 2018 and beyond?

Take serious stock in yourself, your people and what they need from you to grow.

Plan with discipline. After taking stock of what players could do well and not so well, we would play to our strengths and avoid our weakness. For each game, Coach Knight determined the other team's strengths and how our players could best neutralize those strengths. We then worked for the entire week on plays and rules that gave us the best chance to win.

Sometimes, players were put in uncomfortable positions, but not out of their skill level. Learning how to play a slightly new role requires repetition, so we repeated those key factors to winning throughout the week in many different scenarios. Practice was intended to be harder than the actual game.

Similarly, you need to plan your client marketing and interactions with the same discipline. Too often, we think placing products and talking with clients is "selling or marketing." I argue that we have to set aside time and dedicate resources to disciplined marketing to our intended audience. You have to schedule time to network, work on scripts for advertisements, complete video shoots, rehearse radio shows and plan for client events on a regular basis.

Once engaged with a specific client, we have to use a disciplined, repeatable and consistent review process to make best interest recommendations. Just like planning for a new team the next weekend, you have to plan the same way for the next client. Solutions and recommendations will be specific to the client, just like playing against a different team requires different tactics.

Prepare to Win. Winning 30 games during the 1987 season required a lot more detail than this blog allows. However, I think that Coach Knight followed a similar process every year. I've tried to follow a similar process in business as well. I set high, yet realistic goals, know my strengths and weaknesses for those goals and where I have to improve, and execute a consistent game plan that works toward my goals, knowing each situation is different.

Winning Strategy: My favorite quote in sports is, "Everyone has a will to win; few have a will to prepare to win." I always took this lesson to heart from my time with Coach Knight. Apply it to business for success in 2018.

How to Deliver Value and Better Your Business

October 12, 2017

As you read this, the financial services world is changing. While regulatory pressure accelerated a shift over the past 12 months, the current state of fiduciary status was inevitable. Our clients were beginning to demand it, and today, we have to deliver it to even stay in the game.

The challenge, and the main reason to really think about your business in 2018, is to remain relevant with your clients and prospects through the fiduciary standard. The firms that grow will be the ones that not only adapt to the fiduciary rule, but also find ways to differentiate themselves from the rest of the fiduciaries in the marketplace.

Discovering Your True Value

Your value in the marketplace will never be defined by your broker-dealer or regulation. Value is determined by how much you deliver above the cost of your services. That's not to say that the U.S. Department of Labor's rule won't affect how broker-dealers form your commission schedules. But, your level of commission doesn't determine your value. It's how much you deliver to your clients.

Value is about the client experience. How you deliver your expertise may be more meaningful than the information itself. Clients want to have information now. It must be accurate. It has to be timely. And, it must be easy to understand and digest.

Value is also delivered by those items that clients truly value. Asset allocation is becoming – or has been for some time – a commodity. It has become outsourced by third-party money managers, computerized and easy to access via the internet. In order to drive value above your current pricing, you need to find other topics that are important to your clients.

Retirement income is a nearly irrevocable decision. You only get one chance to get it right. If your client begins running out of money, it's usually too late to correct the path. Income planning requires expertise, tools and understanding of the emotional impacts of a variety of external factors. Robo-advisors are not equipped to handle this in-depth conversation and complex problem.

Bettering Your Business

This is where you need to plan for 2018 and beyond – by reshaping your business for maximum success in the future. It's no longer OK to simply bring on new clients, apply an asset allocation model and monitor the assets. You have to think about the demographic shift happening in the United States and the impact on your planning in order to stay ahead.

If you are going to drive value – the ability to give more than you receive from your clients – you have to offer more. That doesn't mean offering more services. It means identifying what's important to your clients and delivering with the best client experience possible.

You need to evaluate the technology, products, services and processes that will guide you and your clients through the discovery and planning process. Look at the talent level in your office to deliver on the changing needs of your clients, and find partners who can assist in delivering new solutions. Taking a step back and looking at your office in the fourth quarter can make a huge difference for many years to come.

Winning Strategy: When setting goals and planning for next year, take a deeper look. Evaluate your process, talent level, technology and client experience. Make sure you are making a difference that adds value to your clients' overall client experience.

4 Trends that will be Critical to Your Practice

October 19, 2017

Right now, clients are demanding that we have their best interests in mind. And, rightfully so. Unfortunately, many consultants and outside counsel tell our industry that best interests translate to level fees and lower commissions. While you may be feeling the effects of leveled commissions, it's no reason to stop growing your business.

Many commission-based products are well suited for clients in the retirement income planning space. And, there are some major demographic shifts taking place that will affect them over the next several decades. The proper combination of assets under management (fees), advice (advisory practice) and commissionable products can create best-interest solutions for many Americans feeling the impact of these trends.

The Trend: Our savings rate has continued to fall over the last two generations. Today, the savings rate rests around 5.0-5.5 percent. We only see spikes in the savings rate during high inflationary periods or when we completely distrust Wall Street. The result, according to the LIMRA Fact Book, is that trailing baby boomers (age 50-59) have saved a median retirement account balance of $130,100.[1]

The Impact: You will have to generate more income with fewer assets than any planning generation before.

The Trend: Americans continually misuse our Social Security system. More than half of Americans take Social Security early – only 2 percent of men, and 4 percent of women, defer their income to age 70.[2] That means nearly 98 percent of men and 96 percent of women are missing out on 8 percent guaranteed growth on their income between full retirement age and age 70. More than half the population takes their income earlier than full retirement age and elects to take as much as 25 percent less in income.

The Impact: You must provide solutions to bridge the gap of income and maximize social programs for your clients.

The Trend: Defined benefit pension plans are being replaced with defined contribution plans. The loss of guaranteed income in a retirement plan will prove devastating over long periods of time. Our research shows that retirement is optimized (95 percent probability of having at least $1 in the portfolio at age 95) with anywhere between 15-25 percent of the portfolio dedicated to producing guaranteed income.

The Impact: You must inform clients that guaranteed income can only come from Social Security, defined benefit pension plans and insurance company contracts (annuities).

The Trend: Longevity risk must be mitigated in order to have a successful retirement strategy. Our spending taper in the United States mirrors a smile more than anything else. Retirees tend to travel in early retirement followed by a slowdown period of spending. At the end of life, there are health concerns, long-term care events and housing elections that increase spending. It's this final phase that is unpredictable, uncapped and highly inflationary, making it difficult to address without proper planning.

The Impact: You must help your clients plan for longevity, or their spending smile will turn into a scowl very quickly.

All of the above are major shifts that are either taking place now, or will affect our business over the next several decades. You have to make sure you can address these issues in your planning practice, regardless of your business model (advisory or commissions). It will be critically important to do more with fewer assets, maximize Social Security, create guaranteed income streams and take the longevity risk off the table. These risks can be mitigated with assets under management and complementary commission-based products. Plan differently to address the shifts that are taking place in America, and grow your business with solutions-based recommendations that include all products.

Winning Strategy: Plan differently to think differently in the future. There are major demographic shifts occurring in the United

States that will affect planning over the next two decades. Get your arms around them now to stay above the crowd in the future.

The Question that Raised the Hair on My Neck … and Can Raise Your Business Standards
October 26, 2017

Early on in my career, I participated in training for wholesalers that emphasized the need to create a business plan with each of my top advisors.

The plan was not complicated. In fact, it was bare-bones, simple and to the point. It established a commitment between me (the wholesaler) and the retail representative, outlining how each expected certain activities from the other to make the relationship mutually beneficial. It was never more than a single page.

Sounds easy, right? Well, it required me to ask the advisor a new question. Changing habits can be hard … but I knew I had to try.

Taking the First Step

After the training, I went out into the field. I had doubts about the value of making a quarterly business plan with each one of my top producers. However, as a new wholesaler with the company that sponsored the training, I felt compelled, even obligated, to try it.

When I arrived at my next meeting, I took nothing other than my pad of paper. The advisor and I talked about her business for about 45 minutes. I learned a lot by asking the right thought-provoking questions, and I gave her some ideas that I thought she might use, based on her business and clientele. This advisor sat in a bank and during my time at her desk, I discovered she did millions of dollars of business with a competitor.

As we wrapped things up, it was time for me to ask her for the next appointment and for us to sit down and do a business plan together. A "yes" meant she liked the interaction with me and my company, and had interest in our products for her clients. A "no" meant I destroyed the relationship before it even got off the ground.

In the past, I would have asked for the next appointment but with no specific purpose. Or, I would have relied on my internal partner to follow up with the advisor and set another follow-up appointment. But, I had made a commitment to myself to change the way I sold – times were changing, and advisors were looking for better partners.

So I gathered up my confidence and asked for the next meeting in three weeks, when I would be back in the area. And, I asked that we set aside 90 minutes to jointly create a business plan that would help keep both of us accountable to reaching some of the goals she had outlined.

There was dead silence for what seemed like an eternity. I could feel the hairs on the back of my neck standing up, and it felt like I was about to break out in a cold sweat.

Her response? She was happy to do it. In fact, she said she didn't move forward with a wholesaler before making a formal business plan with the company's representatives. I was floored. It was as if it was set up by the training school.

Planning for Success

This advisor went on to become a multimillion-dollar producer for me. In our business plan, we agreed to set out the very next quarter to host a client event, where she would have 50 clients and prospects in attendance. In the following quarters, I would provide training to her staff and mailers to use with existing clients, and I would host a networking event for centers of influence around town. For those commitments, she said she anticipated placing a portion of her business with me and my company.

I encourage all financial professionals to have this same requirement of their partners and distributors. As we move deeper into the fiduciary world, it's more important to surround yourself with firms, wholesalers and other advisors whom you can trust with your clients.

Business planning comes in many forms, but planning with your partners might be the most crucial aspect for the ongoing support you need in this complicated financial services world.

Winning Strategy: Create a business plan with each of your vendors. Those who complete the exercise with you should be considered partners. That's what you are looking for in today's complex distribution. You need partners who understand your business and can help it grow.

Make Your Clients 'Smile': Longevity is a Cash Flow Issue
November 2, 2017

Long-term care is an important topic to be sure. However, many industry experts and advisors concentrate on traditional long-term care insurance or linked benefit products. Let's focus on the real problem: Long-term care problem is a cash flow issue, not so much a capital issue.

Extended care expenses can vary widely due to the length of care, severity of condition and level of care required. In reality, these expenses are paid more commonly through cash flow and not capital. If you are using large amounts of capital, you're likely beginning a downward spiral. Things like basic living expenses, income for the healthier spouse or any luxuries become burdensome. The solution is having a suitable and sustainable cash flow for long-term care needs.

Now, you can argue insurance provides the necessary capital to generate that income. It's true. But, rarely do you pay for long-term care in single lump sums to the providers. You need a steady source of guaranteed income that can be flexible enough to turn on and off in order to accommodate those changing expenses.

Smiling Income

Longevity, specifically long-term care, generates a "smile" of expenses. Early in retirement, most people travel and visit friends and family. In the next phase, most retirees see a period of slowing down where they stay closer to home and have fewer expenses. Finally, end-of-life issues arise with unpredictable health care costs. Longevity is not a linear line but more of a smile – and it can become a scowl very quickly if you don't address it.

In order to create cash that resembles a smile, you can prepare clients with guaranteed income now and later through the help of annuities.

Inflation protection can come from assets under management with equities historically outpacing inflation. Additionally, income can be further supported with guaranteed cost-of-living adjustments. This can further reduce the risk on the investment portfolio and its required distribution percentage.

So, when planning for long-term care with a client, think about cash flow, not capital. By focusing on the "smile" of retirement and providing income flexibility, you can address a major concern and offset longevity risks. By having the right amount of income, your client can rest easy, knowing their care will be taken care of and their healthier spouse will not have to experience a change in lifestyle.

Winning Strategy: Create flexibility and control when it comes to income planning for long-term care. Think about cash flow, not capital, when it comes to mitigating longevity risks. While insurance provides the capital, you need to be able to provide income for varying needs.

Why You Shouldn't Wait to Plan for Long-Term Care

November 9, 2017

Aside from running out of money, a long-term care event may be the largest threat to your client's retirement plan. An extended care event can devastate a balance sheet and a family's cash flow. More importantly, it adds unnecessary stress for the retiree, their caregiver and their family.

I'm not suggesting that everyone go out and buy long-term care insurance. Although insurance is the best risk-transfer agent ever developed for situations like this, the reality is not everyone can afford or have access to the proper risk mitigation. But that doesn't mean you can't have a reasonable plan. What's important is that everyone is on the same page and the individual receives the best care possible.

So many times, we get calls for placing assets in other names or entities in an effort to qualify for Medicaid. While that is an effective strategy, I think you need to keep your clients in the front of your mind and provide the best possible care. You need a plan to do that. Planning doesn't hold value when it's time to execute. Planning holds value when you maximize options. You can only do that BEFORE the time of need.

Ask Questions, Find Answers

Talking to your clients about long-term care risk requires a holistic view. Many of our inbound calls possess transactional-level detail about a client. In order to best serve the client, advisors need to dig deeper than the balance sheet.

You have to ask:

- What level of care does the client want in the event of a short-term or long-term event?
- If there is a chronic diagnosis, what type of care can the family caregiver provide and up to what point?
- Where does the client want to live? (This is one of the most under-discussed aspects of retirement and longevity planning.)
- Which assets can be used most effectively now and at the time of the care event?

There are avenues that can help alleviate longevity risks like long-term care. Home equity conversion mortgages provide access to tax-free funds based on the value of the home, annuities and income riders create increasing cash flow for long-term care, and housing facilities can provide a lifetime estate.

Obviously, transferring the entire risk to an insurance company provides the best protection, but chances are that many of your clients will need alternative plans. Planning can make a difference, even just a few years before a care event. Talk to your clients about deploying some of their assets to address a risk that might devastate their plan in the future.

Winning Strategy: Planning doesn't hold any value at the time of execution. Planning adds value when you maximize options. Look at the options now, before your client needs extended care. Address one of the largest risks that can devastate a retiree's plan and transfer the risk as much as possible.

Non-Insurance Options for Long-Term Care Risk

November 16, 2017

Most clients wait too long before addressing longevity and long-term care. They reach a point in their lives when it becomes apparent that they, or people around them, will need care. Unfortunately, at that point, many find the cost of transferring this risk to an insurance company is unaffordable. That's when I think you should devote more resources to the problem.

I realize many Americans have not planned enough to feel secure about their retirement, let alone a long-term care event. But, these concerns can be mitigated through the use of guaranteed income strategies. As I've said before, long-term care is as much of a cash flow issue as it is an insurance or capital issue.

There are many options available to most consumers that are free of underwriting or have reduced underwriting. Annuities provide alternatives to income that are free of medical underwriting yet must meet best-interest standards for clients. These vehicles provide tax-efficient income, longevity protection through lifetime income and the ability to hedge the cash-flow increase due to health concerns.

Income riders allow a client to produce guaranteed minimum levels of income, which can be withdrawn when they need it the most – at the time of a care event. Otherwise, the asset continues to grow tax-deferred, which allows for the account value to grow faster than a normal nonqualified asset.

Deferred income products can allow flexibility in the timing of the disbursement so that your client may turn on the income at a specific period or range of time.

Exclusion ratios can allow for part of the income to be returned to the client tax-free – it's a return of their original basis in the contract. By having some of their income on a tax-free basis, the client may not have to forfeit as much of their account balance.

Guaranteed income can play an important role in mitigating

long-term care expenses, especially for the uninsurable or those who can't afford to shift their risk to an insurer. When you have a client declined for coverage or rated to a point where they will not accept the offer, don't let the risk go unaddressed. Take the initiative to position guaranteed income in the proper light and reduce the cash flow risk.

Winning Strategy: Guaranteed income not only helps with retirement income, but also reduces the risks of long-term care expenses. Don't ignore the risks of clients who can't be covered through insurance.

Turning Tax-Deferred into Tax-Free

November 22, 2017

One of our most successful webinars this year featured two ideas for turning tax-deferred income into tax-free benefits. It's easy to understand the excitement around the topic as there is a large, blue ocean of opportunity for financial advisors who focus on nonqualified annuity sales and the industry's book of business.

According to the 2016 LIMRA Fact Book, there are approximately $468 billion of nonqualified, tax-deferred annuities in the United States. These contracts aren't being used for annuitized, lifetime income. When you peel back the onion, you'll see 31 percent of those contract holders are older than 75, and 68 percent are classified as affluent, high net worth or mega-millionaires by LIMRA. That pairs the industry down to about $100 billion of annuities with a tax-deferred explosion ready to happen at death of the owner.*

With long-term care as a huge risk in the longevity plan for retirement, it's important to consider options for those annuities. Those idle assets are no longer needed for their original purpose: income. Instead, they are being conserved and protected to be passed on to the next generation.

A Better Way

Using a tax-free exchange under IRC Section 1035, the client may exchange the old annuity for a linked-benefit annuity. This transfer benefits the client in several ways:

- The new product captures all the gain in the old policy. If the old annuity was connected to variable sub accounts, now might be a good time to "lock in" those gains using a fixed contract like a linked benefit annuity.

- Clients gain leverage on the policy's value if used for long-term care expenses. For a 65-year-old, a $100,000 policy value may create a pool of long-term care benefits of $250,000 or more. This translates to transferring $1 and getting $2.50 when used for long-term care. You create tremendous leverage through this transfer.

- If the old policy had tax-deferred gains built in, those gains are transferred and continue to grow on a tax-deferred basis. If the contract is used for qualified long-term care expense, all the proceeds – the cost basis and the gain – are received tax-free.

Look at your client's balance sheet and the current purpose of certain assets. A lot of them aren't being used for their original intent. Now is a great opportunity to repurpose those assets and create leverage and value in the planning process.

Winning Strategy: Look to turn tax-deferred income into tax-free benefits. A great way to add value to your relationships is by repurposing assets that are no longer meeting client goals. By looking at old annuities, you may be able to reduce the tax burden to the client and their beneficiaries.

LIMRA, Fact Book on Retirement Income 2016: https://www.limra.com/bookstore/item_details.aspx?sku=23518-001

Why Longevity is a Crucial Factor in Retirement Planning

November 30, 2017

Longevity can mean different things to different people. We want to think that it signifies a long life, an active lifestyle and remaining relevant in our communities as we age. Reality has a different take on longevity. For many Americans, longevity remains an unknown risk with unknown costs.

Longevity creates a spending "smile." Here's how it looks:

- Retirees start out their golden years traveling and visiting with family and friends – enjoying their retirement.
- Often, they begin to slow down. Rarely is it because they want to. Instead, their energy levels and health begin to take a front seat to their vision of retirement. They stay home more frequently and follow a routine.
- Finally, in too many situations, their health deteriorates to a point where they need additional care services. The retirement they planned for – both figuratively and financially – is off course, and there is little chance of pulling it back.

Risks are all over the place during retirement. A growing number of Americans need extended care, either at home or in a facility, which costs thousands on a monthly basis. Our savings rate continues to decline, placing pressure on whether clients will run out of income during retirement. General health care expenses remain an unknown and a topic which will surely change several times during a retirement span. Simply put, we cannot ignore the risks of living too long.

Start Talking

As planners, we owe it to our clients to have a conversation about longevity. By planning ahead, you give your clients options that can't be offered at the time of the need. Risks can be mitigated using guaranteed income, shifting the risk to an insurance product, or through proper distribution planning.

It's easy to simply apply a distribution percentage and assume a rate of return. That's why we have software – to do the easy stuff. But, our value can't be brought down to the level of a software package. Our value as planners is to think critically about our client's situation and help them meet challenges – those they are aware of and those that are not present today. That requires making sure there is enough income to meet the demands of longevity.

We have to make sure our clients can transition from accumulation to distribution. The rules are dramatically different for these phases of life. Take time to discuss the client's vision of retirement, the duration, the standard of living, and potential risks that might get in the way. Hit those risks head on. It will provide confidence and peace of mind to your client. And, at the end of the day, that is one of your largest value propositions to your clients and prospects.

Winning Strategy: Longevity means a lot of different things. Make sure you have a clear picture of what longevity is and what risks come into play. Hitting those risks head on can mean the difference between success and failure for many Americans in retirement.

Safety in Numbers: 3 Reasons to Stop Running with the Crowd

December 7, 2017

When we have a market correction – and we will have one sooner or later – many investors will run to banks and place their assets in money market accounts or certificates of deposit (CDs). While those are traditional safe havens for many people, they tend to be temporary. Once the markets start rising again, investors leave their safe havens to take on more risk.

We need to rethink why we do those transactions and if it's worth the effort to complete the run to safety. Instead, why not think about proper allocation for a risk tolerance that probably can't stomach the full amount risk being taken.

As the old saying goes ...

You never know how much risk to take until you take too much.

Rethinking Risk Strategies

A temporary shift in risk management does very little for clients in the long run. There are several reasons, but here are three.

1. Money markets and CDs earn historically low interest rates compared to instruments like annuities. Today, the average annuity is earning 200 to 250 bps more for A-rated carriers on a five-year product. Now, liquidity is not equal – bank accounts are generally liquid, while CDs have some type of penalty if not held to maturity. Annuities provide liquidity in emergencies and limited free withdrawals. Remember, we are talking about rethinking allocations to avoid the temporary run toward safety. In a new allocation strategy, liquidity would likely come from other assets first.

2. Taxation favors annuities. Even during the high tax rates and high inflation/return periods of the late '70s and early '80s, tax-deferred assets outperformed their taxable counterparts. Not only in return, but mainly in real return – after tax, inflation and fees.

3. There is a common misconception that money market accounts can't lose money. In fact, they do fluctuate in value and can go below their targeted $1 valuation. With many annuities, the client receives a guarantee of principal plus a minimum interest rate return.

Safety can come in many forms. The most popular are bank instruments, which serve a great purpose. However, the numbers point toward a better solution: better nominal and real rates of return, lower tax rates and more stable values. Add in the fact that charges are not paid upfront and occur only when you do not hold the asset to maturity. This makes the purchase efficient from a cost perspective, an effective way to increase yields on conservative vehicles and provide confidence to the client by showing them a more stable valuation of their conservative asset selection.

Winning Strategies: Don't follow the leader or the crowd when the market corrects. Rethink your current allocation strategies and look at the real returns to help clients protect their wealth in the most efficient way possible.

Making the Comeback Count

December 14, 2017

Everyone loves a comeback. How many times have you watched a sporting event where the losing team suddenly comes from behind? It doesn't matter the sport – at that point, nearly everyone cheers for the underdogs.

As thrilling as it is, many comebacks end in disappointment. The losing team expends so much energy and effort in the comeback, they don't have enough left in their tanks to win.

Seems familiar, doesn't it?

Are you preparing your clients for
a retirement comeback but a shortfall in the end?

Sometimes, we have to help clients make a comeback – they didn't save enough during their working years to get the income they were hoping for. You have to come to their rescue so they can "catch up." Even if they did save enough, we too often focus on just getting them to the goal line. Great – now, it's time to finish the game.

Unfortunately, many people get seven to 10 years into retirement and realize that they have fallen short in their plan. Inflation begins to take a toll on their spending. Most notably, the cost of health care increases at a rate much faster than other goods and services, putting pressure on them to make adjustments. By planning ahead – looking beyond just "catching up" or making it to retirement – you can help position both guaranteed income and inflation protection.

Winning the Game

One of the easiest ways to mitigate inflation is to push Social Security to age 70. Social Security typically has an inflation component that increases the income annually, even if at a slower rate than other inflation indices. Other income sources provide guaranteed options to increase the monthly income by 1-5 percent annually, and riders allow the income to increase by changes in the underlying crediting method. Either way, by increasing the client's income, you have helped push them closer to the top of winning their income game – longevity and inflation.

Winning Strategy: Don't be like the teams that get behind early and spend too much energy coming back, only to lose in the end. Make sure your clients win with inflation protection in addition to guaranteed income.

Avoiding Derailment

December 21, 2017

Let me ask you something …

What's the one thing that can completely derail a near-retiree's plan?

Many answers might come to mind. But, I'm willing to bet most of them revolve around the reliability of market returns. Think of your clients' journey like a train on a long-distance trip – if you're not careful, you could derail them just before their destination.

Starting Up: As your clients travel through their working years, they sit in the conductor's seat. Most don't have a lot of disposable income in the early years – anything they make goes to pay the bills, and not much is left for long-term savings. As they work through their careers, they begin earning more money and committing more to their retirement. The locomotive starts to build steam and momentum.

Slowing Down: Market corrections are inevitable. Your clients' trains will have to slow down every now and then. But, that's OK – most plans account for slow-downs, and there's usually plenty of time to pick up speed. Once assured that the difficulties are behind, you can increase speed and head back on track. Sometimes, you even need to switch to a more aggressive line to make up lost time.

Picking Up Speed: When we continue along a journey with few to no problems, it's easy to forget about the fundamentals of steering a train. You can easily go too fast around a corner. If you're not careful, the momentum you built can work against you. After years of picking up speed, your locomotive and the cars behind it can derail and spin out of control, completely stopping you in your tracks.

Avoiding Derailment: That's what happens when we have a late-accumulation market correction. All the cars – retirement income, emergency funds, health care payments, long-term care plans – they all go off track of what we planned. The momentum your client has built for 30-plus years is ruined. But, it can all be avoided if we steer them the right way.

You have a lot of clients with their eyes firmly focused on their final destination – retirement. Unfortunately, that means they sometimes take their eyes off the track they're headed down. You can really make a difference for those clients now and during the distribution phase. You can help conduct the train and get it safely down the tracks.

Winning Strategies: Ash Brokerage answers the complex questions you and your clients have in preparation for retirement. Begin by talking to your clients about the need to be more conservative and avoid the risks that can derail retirement at the end of their journey.

How You Can Find Safety in Guaranteed Income
December 28, 2017

Our headquarters is at the heart of Fort Wayne, Indiana, a city that was severely hurt by the downturn of the automobile and manufacturing sectors. But today, it's seeing a resurgence, especially downtown. Our building, the Ash Skyline Plaza, is about 18 months old, and a 15-story complex, Skyline Tower, is being built adjacent to us – just across the rooftop park.

I can see all the construction activity from my office – many times, I have to turn and look away so I can concentrate. There's nothing like a portable toilet flying up on a crane to make you lose your train of thought.

But, I admire those workers. They're onsite before I arrive and still there long after I leave, even on the weekends. It's tough work, for sure. And, it's dangerous, plain and simple. But the crew members all wear safety harnesses, hard hats and boots to protect themselves. It's part of their everyday habits.

That makes me think …

What safety habits are you instilling in your clients?

As they build their portfolios and retirement income, your clients are taking risks. Many of those risks are associated with longevity or outliving their income:

- Market returns
- Sequence of returns
- Inflation
- Long-term care events
- Legacy planning constraints
- Taxes

Regardless of what happens with all those risks, the safety harness is income. As long as a client has income, they will likely feel more comfortable, regardless of what risks arise. Now, those risks still have to be addressed. But, if your client can feel confident that their income is secure from market drops and inflation, you have a good chance at addressing the other risks.

We have to instill safe habits when it comes to retirement income planning. Nearly everyone can benefit from having guaranteed income as part of their retirement plan. Whether it's from defined benefit plans, Social Security or insurance company annuities, guaranteed income shifts the risks of longevity. However, only one of those sources has embedded inflation protection, so you must address inflation with your client. Income serves as a great safety harness for those taking investment risks.

Winning Strategy: Focus on the risks that longevity creates for your clients. If you address their fears and concerns, you are likely to win a client for life, as well as many quality referrals.

The First 5 Minutes: How to Set a Positive Tone for Your Entire Year

January 4, 2018

No matter the sport, there are a few critical points in every game when coaches focus on motivating their teams. Obviously, finishing the game strong is a must – you have to execute down the stretch and perform in pressure situations.

However, coaches also talk about the first five minutes of each half as being critical to success. The first five minutes set the tone, allow the team to put pressure on the opponent and energize (or take out) the crowd.

As we begin 2018, I think the first five minutes of your year are important for the same reasons. You have to set the tone for your clients, relieve them of the pressures of retirement income planning and take out some of the risks of retirement, namely longevity issues. Each has a specific purpose in helping your clients feel more confident in their long-term retirement strategy. By focusing on your clients' needs, you add tremendous value to their lives.

- What are some events that might derail your clients' retirement today?
- If you could reduce that risk, how much value would your client feel you delivered?

Set the Tone

Could a correction happen in 2018 or 2019? Are your clients able to time the market to avoid an eventual correction? With today's rising equity markets, it's hard to take investments out of the market.

We have a tendency to maximize the returns for our clients each and every year. However, as they age, return is less important to many as their focus turns to income versus accumulation. Our clients fear they will not have enough income in retirement, and our response is mistakenly to accumulate more assets. In reality, we have to protect their asset base and help them generate more income.

Lock in Gains

Our clients have accumulated trillions of dollars of assets in qualified plans. The current tax law allows for qualified transfers from one individual retirement account (IRA) to a rollover IRA with no current tax as long as it meets the transfer criteria, i.e., direct trustee-to-trustee transfer.

By using conservative vehicles to sweep gains from their account, the client can take investment risk off the table while earning a competitive, conservative return. In many cases, the client can still earn indexing credits tied to their favorite equity or blended allocation index up to 5 or 6 percent (current pricing as of January 2018). If the client sweeps the gain from their mutual fund or accumulation-based variable annuity, they have "locked in" the gains from the previous bull run.

If the markets continue to increase, they can participate in some of the equity returns up to the stated maximum cap or participation rate, and they won't lose the gains they have built.

Your clients will enjoy knowing that if a market correction comes in 2018, you have protected their gains and positioned them for success. A 20 percent correction may take years to recover, and many of our trailing baby boomer clients (age 50-59) cannot afford a dip in their assets just prior to retirement.

Winning Strategy: Locking in gains from the recent long bull run allows you to set a positive tone for your clients in 2018. It takes pressure off their decision of when to exit the stock market. They'll be able to participate in equity indexing, and you can maintain positive momentum for income in the event of a market correction.

3 Ideas to Quickly Generate Profit

January 5, 2018

If you're like me, you run a business. And, you do so for profit – for you or for your stakeholders.

Profit can be summarized by an income statement showing gross revenue, expenses and net profit. But, I think it's broken down to two factors: effectiveness and efficiency. The better you can execute on these factors, the greater your profit will be. In order to do that, you have to work smarter, finding ways to generate top-line revenue while minimizing client acquisition costs.

One of the fastest ways to generate new revenue is to capture a greater share of your clients' wallets – or more market share of household investments. Creating a new stream of income from existing clients drastically reduces the cost of acquiring a new relationship.

But how do you create additional revenue without exposing your assets?

- First, repurposing old assets makes sense as you position your clients for retirement. Many have changed jobs throughout their careers and let assets simply accumulate in former employers' qualified plans or individual retirement accounts. Those assets should be considered for lifetime income assets. By positioning guaranteed income in the portfolio, you can reallocate the assets under management to meet longer term goals, as well as gain tax efficiency and the potential for growth. If positioned properly, many of these assets can be placed on trail-based compensation to create recurring income for your financial practice.
- Second, many old assets have beneficiary designations that have not been reviewed. Our firm commissioned a white paper by a respected ERISA attorney that identifies the risks of qualified plan beneficiaries. Taking the time to review and

rename beneficiaries can save a family thousands of dollars in income taxes when the asset transfers to the next generation. By leveraging this savings, you have the potential to gain the confidence of the next generation. So, reviewing asset beneficiaries has the effect of repurposing the asset as well as creating a bridge to future clients.

- Third, as our clients near retirement, many will want to take Social Security. Using an unused asset to create a bridge has proven to be a positive move for many clients. The bridge – in the form of a single-premium immediate annuity – allows the client to receive the same income as an early election from Social Security. However, the strategy generates more than $122,000 more in income from age 70 to 90. The increased leverage from social programs protects assets under management and allows for a positive conversation with the next generation as well.

Looking within your own client base makes your business more efficient. Your existing clients provide the fastest path to new revenues – many of which can be recurring.

With so many Americans afraid of running out of money in retirement, you have a chance to provide assurances that your clients will maintain the standard of living they are planning for. When your activities focus on ways to be effective and efficient, the chance of increasing your profits grows exponentially.

Winning Strategy: To draw profit for your business, look inward. You will earn more business from your existing clients with quality ideas. This creates additional revenue, plus opportunities to be introduced to the next generation.

One of the Easiest Decisions
You Can Make for Your Clients

January 11, 2018

Clients have a lot going on at the start of the year. Work brings new challenges and new budget constraints. Kids go to college and start a new semester, which brings the returned stress of tuition. And, they've probably deferred a conversation with you, their planner, because they were too busy in December. Now it seems they are just as busy, if not busier.

So many things go on in other aspects of your clients' lives that you have to make their financial decisions easy. You can address longevity concerns, making at least one decision easier and less painful amidst all the distractions swirling around them.

Tax-Deferred to Tax-Free?

We're always trying to minimize taxes for our clients. Unfortunately, some of our products create a tax at death that is higher than if we had not placed it in a tax-deferred instrument to begin with. According to LIMRA's 2017 Fact Book, there are $486 billion in nonqualified assets on insurance carriers' books that are not providing income to their owners. Amazingly, a large percentage of those clients are over age 75 and considered affluent or mega-millionaires.

If those are your clients, they have a potentially severe problem. How can you better leverage an asset that isn't being used for its intended purpose?

Current tax law allows a 1035 exchange from one annuity to another with continued tax deferral. Better yet, if you transfer the asset to an approved asset-based LTC annuity, the proceeds are accessible tax free when used for qualified long-term care expenses. Where else can you transfer a tax-deferred gain to a tax-free distribution under the proper scenario? "Rothification" requires claiming the gain as a taxable gain in the current year. By concentrating on nonqualified assets, you can continue to defer the gain and potentially access it tax free.

When you propose this type of transfer, the client benefits in several ways:

- The asset continues to grow tax deferred and they have no taxable gain on the transfer
- The client creates leverage from the purchase of the long-term care annuity as the carrier provides a tax-free pool of assets for long-term care expenses
- If the client needs long-term care, they access the cost basis and the gain in the policy without any tax consequences

Your practice benefits from this conversation in several ways:

- You preserve and protect your assets under management from one of the costliest expenses in longevity planning
- You generate another source of revenue from an asset that was likely not creating revenue for the firm, or you capture more assets from a previous financial planning firm
- Because you helped the family and generated capital when they need it most, you have a greater chance of working with the next generation

Look at your existing clients and ask about their nonqualified assets. The opportunity is large and can help relieve their longevity concerns immensely.

Winning Strategy: There is a large opportunity ready to be transferred to the next generation. If you provide a better transfer path and better tax consequences, you will win business and clients.

2 Investment Theories that are Critical in Today's Market

January 18, 2018

When you're done reading this, you should Google "investment theory." You will find more than 577 million articles, videos, news releases and opinions about thousands of investment theories. It's mind-boggling to think of all the different ways you can manage assets in this industry.

The problem is we forget the most important part of managing assets is ensuring our client understands and feels comfortable with the direction of their portfolio. Maybe even more important is how our clients make decisions.

Out of the millions of Google results, there are two theories that I find relevant in today's investment management market: Prospect Theory and Recency Bias. Understanding how your clients react to these two behavioral theories is important in how you manage their expectations and set the course for their retirement strategies.

Recency Bias assumes you are going to get the same result as you had previously when there is a chain of consistent events. For example, if you watch a football game and the kicker is setting up for a game-winning field goal, you assume he will make it because of his high percentage of successful kicks and the fact that he already kicked several field goals earlier in the game. In reality, he has no better chance of hitting that field goal than any other kick. But, our recency bias tells us that he will make it. In investing, the recent gains in just about every asset class make us think that the equity and bond markets will continue to increase. In reality, there is no fundamental reason to believe that the chances of continued equity market increases are greater than they have ever been. We just perceive that the markets will go up. Our clients feel the same way when they make decisions.

Prospect Theory addresses the willingness to avoid loss. In most cases, clients feel a loss 2.25 times more than the same amount of gain. They tend to choose products on how they are positioned. For example, let's assume that the total return for a client in two different scenarios is $25 for the same, two-year fixed period. One results in a steady gain of $25 over the two years, or $12.50 for each year. Another scenario allows the client to achieve a $50 gain in year one but a $25 loss in year two, resulting in the same net $25. Most clients tend to choose the first scenario because they have a tendency to look for gains and avoid losses, even if the result is the same.

As we look into 2018, think about how your clients might be affected by different market scenarios. How likely are they to get scared or concerned if they don't see the steady growth of their retirement dollars? Is your practice in a better position by ensuring your clients feel better about steady growth versus random fluctuations in the market? Make sure you understand what your clients are feeling in order to build the portfolio that best matches their goals.

Winning Strategy: Understanding how clients react to recent events and potential gains and losses is just as important as managing money to benchmarks. Take time to ask the right questions and look at alternatives to address behavior and money management theories.

Why You Should Transfer Risk to Transform Your Business

January 25, 2018

A successful 2018 can come in the form of multiple opportunities. Some will happen fast, while others will require an investment of your time, money and energy. But, the latter are opportunities that tend to transform your business and provide exponential growth. You need to think about both – creating quick results while making strides for long-term growth.

If you are going to make 2018 your best year ever, think about changing the way you talk with clients. We tend to think about performance, rates of return and fees. Those are important items, but the transfer of risk can be more important on several levels.

Why would you want to retain risk without any larger return for doing so?

Help Clients Keep an Income

The answer is usually the cost of the insurance. Many times, our clients choose to self-insure their retirement income through systematic withdrawals of assets under management. You need to help them understand the risks of longevity and the costs of not transferring their risks.

Our research shows that most people, regardless of income and net worth, benefit from having 15 percent of their portfolio from guaranteed income sources. Those sources are Social Security, defined benefit plans and privately purchased annuities. The ability to pool your life expectancy with other people creates a transfer of risk that is not available in any investment vehicle besides guaranteed income sources.

Help Companies Keep Promises

As you meet with business owners, many will want to shift the risks of aging pension plans to another source. There are trillions of dollars in pension plans across the United States that no longer serve their corporations. The plans are not properly rewarding the people for extended service. The plans don't help recruit better talent. And, they aren't accruing additional benefits. They're simply a liability for many CEOs today.

Transferring a pension plan allows a company to free up resources that would normally be used for administrative work on an outdated plan. Due to tax reform, some companies spend idle dollars to sure up their plan. Many are in a great position to transfer to an insurance carrier. While there is a one-year premium to shift this risk, the cost savings of administrating the plan typically outweigh the initial premium.

Winning Strategy: Change your client presentations toward shifting risks. Clients are surrounded by risks in today's retirement planning market. Be different. Returns won't matter if you can shift some of the income risk to an insurance carrier.

How to Create Value Beyond Fees or Returns

February 1, 2018

If you're like most of the people I've talked to over the past 18 months, you've felt revenue compression. As our industry gravitates toward more transparency, it's fair to expect continued reductions on commissions and fees. So, part of becoming a more successful financial planner involves defining your value in a whole new way.

It's no longer enough to have the lowest fees or the best returns – anyone can have the best returns in any given year. According to research from S&P Dow Jones, only 5 percent of active money managers continued beating the index after a three-year run of beating the S&P 500.[1]

Any advisor can lower their fees until they are unprofitable and unsustainable. Go ahead and Google "online financial planning software," and you'll see how low your fees will have to be if you want to compete – free. As Bob Burg and John David Mann explain in "The Go-Giver," you must think about your value in terms of how much you give your client in excess of the payments you receive.[2]

Customize Your Value to Your Clients

Return and fees might be a part of your overall value, but they are no longer the determining factor for clients to select advisors and stay with them. You need to provide additional value to every client on their own terms. Customization is critical. Know what motivates each and every client interaction. Examples might include online access to information, bill paying ability, concierge or complimentary professional services, or family office services.

Understanding what is important to your client is the key to success – it's not a specific investment theory that can ultimately be duplicated. Providing service and expertise that's personalized to their situation adds value. Focusing on the client and delivering what they want adds value. Every. Single. Time.

Your Client-Focused Business Model

The fiduciary standard forces you to walk away from your own interests and place them on your clients. That includes your business model. Your new business model should be "the client model." You should be asking yourself:

- What is the ultimate goal for this client/prospective client?
- What can I do to put the client in a better position financially?
- If my client sat down a year from now and said, "Thank you for making my life better!" what would have happened, and what would I have done with this client?

- How can I help this client the most?

That is a client-focused model. No concern about your upfront or ongoing revenue streams. Did you provide value to the client on their terms? That's the ultimate question you have to answer.

Winning Strategy: Focus on growing your business through a client-focused model. Your true worth in a client relationship is determined by how much you give in value, not what you take in payment.

[1]*S&P Dow Jones Indices, "Fleeting Alpha: Evidence From the SPIVA and Persistence Scorecards," February 2017: http://us.spindices.com/documents/research/research-fleeting-alpha-evidence-from-the-spiva-and-persistence-scorecards.pdf*
[2]*Bob Burg and John David Mann, "The Go-Giver: A Little Story About a Powerful Business Idea": https://thegogiver.com/*

Compensation Shifts

February 8, 2018

The "Law of Compensation" states that your income is directly related to number of people you serve and how well you serve them.* Notice that the law does not claim one business model is better than the next. In fact, business model, e.g., fee-based, commission, etc., is irrelevant to how much compensation you earn.

The key to your success or failure isn't compensation. The key is focus – focus on clients and prospective clients.

No matter your business model, you will dramatically increase your compensation by focusing on the number of people you serve and how well you serve them.

Let's look at the first part: the number of people you serve. Common practice will tell you that less is more. You need to work with a smaller number of clients with high net worths. That's a business model. That model can be scaled to new heights through the investment of para-planners, support staff and additional planners (which makes a great succession plan for the firm). By reinvesting in your business, you can serve more clients and increase your compensation.

The next part is about maintaining value in your service. As you increase your number of clients, it's important not to lose sight of their individual needs, desires and planning objectives. Again, investments in technology, people and infrastructure can make a huge difference.

A Focused Mindset

Your clients hire you to look them in the eye and solve their most complex issues – retirement and longevity. The level of service you provide is more important than the model you use. In fact, rarely do clients ask about your business model. They care about your expertise, how well they will be served, and how much they feel their goals and objectives are a priority.

It's inappropriate to choose a solution for a client based on your business model. You have to change your mindset to focus on your clients and what risks concern them the most. If their concerns are longevity and income, you owe it to them to look at guaranteed income options, even if that is against your business model.

Winning Strategy: Maximize your compensation and revenue by looking at how you can help more people and increase the level of service you provide. Both will elevate your business.

*Bob Burg and John David Mann, "The Go-Giver: A Little Story About a Powerful Business Idea": https://thegogiver.com/

The 2 Keys to Growing Your Influence (and Business)

February 9, 2018

Q: Whom do you consider as part of your network?
A: If it's just your clients and vendors, you're short selling yourself.
Q: How do you gain influence in your network?
A: By focusing on their needs and wants – not your goals.

Influence – in your industry, in your community, with your clients, or within your wider network – requires the same focus that lifts your compensation. Let's break this discussion into two key parts: the focus and your network.

Focus

First, in order to earn influence, you must understand other people's goals and objectives. This understanding isn't just limited to your business. You have to dig deeper in your relationships to have understanding and empathy for whatever is happening in the lives of others. The last part is something I think is a lost art. Our lives are so complex and busy that so many people affect the way people see the world. Our color of lens changes rapidly.

You can really help a lot of people by taking time to understand where they are right now, what's keeping them up at night and what would truly be beneficial to them. It's likely to change frequently. All of this goes back to the "law of value," which states that your worth is determined by how much you give over what you receive.

Network

Second, just like compensation, you need to think of your network as more than the obvious. Think outside of your clients and colleagues – think of people who will become your "brand ambassadors" – people who know you, like you and trust you.* How do you build that trust? You guessed it … by bringing value to the relationship and helping others meet their goals.

Your network is endless. You never know the source of your next referral or an opportunity, so treat everyone as part of your network. Focus the conversation on them and learn how you might help them. In doing so, you quickly build rapport and trust.

Influence Your Future

By doing these two simple steps, you will grow your network abundantly over time, probably quicker than you think. Growing your network is the most efficient way to grow your practice. Stay focused on others and treat every contact as part of your network. Some will be better ambassadors than others. But, don't risk the lost opportunity. Take time to get to know other people and how you can help first. Your value will prevail.

Winning Strategy: In every encounter, concentrate on

understanding the other person. Look to make everyone an ambassador for your planning services by focusing on them, not yourself. This leads to quicker rapport and trust, both of which are essential to referrals.

Bob Burg and John David Mann, "The Go-Giver: A Little Story About a Powerful Business Idea": https://thegogiver.com/

Now is the Best Time to Be … YOU

February 15, 2018

This is the most incredible time in our industry to be a human … any human … well, actually, you! While there is a preponderance of online software, none of it can deliver the value of real, authentic human beings.

Technology competes largely on price. Software can calculate retirement income for less money, or help people manage their own finances for half the cost. But, when you compete on price, you roll the dice. While technology might do some things well, it can't compete with everything you can do as a human advisor.

- You can look people in the eye and talk to them about the harsh realities of longevity
- You can help others overcome emotional roadblocks to improving their savings and income planning
- You can explain how everything will be OK if a spouse dies unexpectedly
- You can protect an entire family and discuss options to transfer business ownerships, retirement plans and long-held family assets
- You can ask insightful questions to find the real reasons a person is investing

Our industry's true value is all of us – the unique individuals who take time to fully understand the needs and desires of clients and prospective clients. As Bob Burg and John David Mann explain in "The Go-Giver," authenticity is your best asset.* Each of us brings a unique talent to the table. You can ill-afford to be another robo-advisor focused on pure numbers, beating the benchmarks by a couple basis points or slightly lower fees.

Your clients want more. They want you. They want someone who will look them in the eye and say, "You are going to be fine. We are going to take care of you." Don't try to compete against a custodian or a large financial institution – just be yourself and you will find people who want that interaction.

Winning Strategy: You are your best asset. Don't try to be something you're not. Surround yourself with people who complete your financial practice. Most importantly, be yourself within your network and in your client interactions. It's your best differentiation.

*Bob Burg and John David Mann, "The Go-Giver: A Little Story About a Powerful Business Idea": https://thegogiver.com/

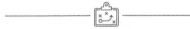

Why You Must Be Willing to Receive in Order to Give

February 22, 2018

The title might seem a little confusing. The concept of being willing to receive is confusing, at best.

All this month, we have talked about the Go-Giver Laws of Stratospheric Success.* All of the Go Giver laws are within our control. The "Law of Receptivity" is no different. Staying open to opportunities might seem easy on the surface, but it might be the most difficult.

Take Notice

When I was a child, my parents bought into the Volkswagen Beetle fad of the early '70s. The little cars were fun to drive and got great gas mileage. I loved the rumble seat in the back of the car where my brother and I rode to kindergarten and grade school. The trunk was in the front of the car while the engine was in the back, so the rumble seat truly rumbled!

The McGlothlin family Volkswagen was a bright orange Beetle. You could see us coming for miles. When dad brought "Herbie" home from the dealership, we thought we had the only orange VW in Indianapolis. But, as we drove around the highway and even around our smaller community in central Indiana, we noticed a lot of orange VW Beetles. I'm sure you can say the same thing for your car. You never really noticed another until you bought one. Then, all of a sudden, they're everywhere.

Being open to receiving is similar. You're always looking out for others, solving their dilemmas and adding value to the relationship. Adding value will always be followed by someone giving to you. You don't recognize it until after it is happening, just like you don't see the orange Beetle until you've bought it.

Breathe Through It

The natural flow of business is an exchange of value. This is usually done in dollars for service or a product. But, receiving is much more than that. Receiving can be a simple "thank you" for doing something special. It can be a mutually beneficial business relationship. It can come in many shapes and sizes, but you'll know it when you receive it. And, you must be willing to receive it in order to continue giving properly. In "The Go-Giver," breathing is used as an analogy for giving and receiving. You must exhale in order to inhale and vice versa.

It's important to always remember that receiving isn't a scoreboard – nothing about the Laws of Stratospheric Success is a scoreboard. You can never count your chips by how much time, energy and value you have provided. You can't think that you are "owed" something in return. Instead, it will flow naturally, maybe even when you least expect it.

Winning Strategy: Be open to success. Don't expect it. Earn it. But always be open to it.

Bob Burg and John David Mann, "The Go-Giver: A Little Story About a Powerful Business Idea": https://thegogiver.com/

Asset Location Over Allocation

March 1, 2018

As I travel back from a business trip to Portland, I'm reminded how important location is on an airplane. Flying four and a half hours in the middle seat is not fun, especially when you don't sleep on an airliner like me.

Over the past few years, the location of assets has become more important in the financial planning arena. The biggest reason is the continued shift to income versus accumulation. During distribution, income is more important than the rate of return, which is largely driven by the allocation of assets. Let's look at an example where location can improve your chances of success.

Average Couple, Average Approach

A typical American couple approaches your firm. They have done a nice job of creating a nest egg for their retirement and would like to receive $50,000 a year in retirement income. They anticipate receiving $20,000 of annual Social Security income. So, they need to take $30,000 a year from their accumulated assets of $750,000. In other words, they will need to sustain a 4 percent withdrawal strategy from their assets under management.

While the 4 percent rule worked during higher interest rate periods, most economists believe the safe withdrawal rate is around 2.8 percent to 3.5 percent. Without a doubt, this couple is in jeopardy of a significant failure in retirement, especially if they were to have a significant drop in asset value early in their retirement years. This is where asset location can make a huge difference over asset allocation. Because allocation doesn't fully protect the clients from a loss in their account – it might make the ride smoother or reduce their losses and gains, but it will not provide protection from losses.

What worked for clients during the accumulation phase will not work for them during the distribution phase. In fact, in many cases, the strategies that clients used to accumulate assets will hurt them in retirement.

New Approach, Better Outcomes

Let's look at using different products to sure up their retirement income.

- First, the couple buys a single-premium immediate annuity (SPIA) to secure $9,000 of annual income. In today's interest rate environment, that will cost just under $170,000 of the account value. The SPIA's income is protected for both the spouses' lives, and if they both die before using up the $170,000, their beneficiaries get the balance of the unused funds.

- Next, the couple purchases a fixed indexed annuity (FIA). The $100,000 FIA generates $5,000 of guaranteed annual income. The clients remain in control of the assets and can change the annuity if something happens.

- Their remaining $480,000 is invested in their asset allocation strategy according to their risk tolerance. The assets only need to create $16,000 of annual income off the $480,000 in assets. That means the use of two additional products reduces the withdrawal percentage to 3.3 percent. Most would agree the 3.3 percent is a significant improvement to the withdrawal percentage and increases the probability of success.

The result is that the clients begin their retirement with the same $50,000 of targeted income:

- $20,000 from Social Security
- $16,000 from the systematic withdrawal strategy
- $9,000 from the SPIA
- $5,000 front the FIA

Notice that between Social Security and the annuities, $34,000 of their $50,000 annual income is guaranteed for the rest of their lives. That makes a powerful impact on their retirement income strategy.

Winning Strategy: Asset location is more important than allocation during the income phase. Look at using alternative income-producing assets to reduce pressure on assets and provide a more secure retirement income.

Digging Deeper: 3 Ways to Generate Revenue from your Existing Book of Business

March 8, 2018

As I travel around the country on business, I enjoy talking with advisors from different channels – banks, broker-dealers, independent agents, registered investment advisors. Regardless of business model or channel, one topic always comes up:

> *"I need to find more clients. Can you help me with*
> *a seminar or dinner so I can find new clients?"*

But, I like to think of the question differently and ask:

> *"Are you interested in finding more clients?*
> *Or more revenue for your practice?"*

Usually, the answer is revenue. But advisors tend to think that new clients are the source of new sales and revenue, which is partly true. However, there's a goldmine of revenue opportunities with your existing clients.

Mine Your Book

According to LIMRA's 2016 Fact Book, there are $486 billion of assets in nonqualified annuities – both variable and fixed – on carriers' books right now. Some facts to consider:

- These contracts are NOT being annuitized, and the owners are NOT electing to receive income from the rider
- Approximately 33 percent of those owners are older than 75; of those owners, 65 percent are classified as affluent, high-net-worth or mega-millionaires – clients who are either in your book of business or being recruited to your firm

To make a difference for the people with whom you already work, I suggest you dig deeper. Look at those older contracts and find a better use than just tax-deferred accumulation. Here are three suggestions:

1. Talk to your clients about putting the IRS in the back of the line, and your clients and their beneficiaries in front. Products today offer an exclusion ratio with the ability to access the cost basis first, without incurring the ordinary income tax immediately at time of death. Then, the beneficiary can spread out the tax consequences for a longer period.

2. Turn tax-deferred assets into tax-free benefits for long-term care purposes. Asset-based long-term care products allow you to transact an exchange without current taxes and continue the tax-deferred growth. If the client uses the funds for qualified long-term care expenses, the cost basis and gains are returned to the client tax-free. You've taken a future tax consequence and turned it into useful and timely tax-free capital.

3. Lock in the gains. We've seen an unprecedented bull market since the financial crisis. Many clients do not want to take as much investment risk as they did 10 years ago. And, when asked about it, they probably don't want to feel the same pain they felt in 2009. Sweep the variable contracts with no downside protection to a more secure vehicle that qualifies for a tax-free exchange, either fixed or fixed indexed. You might want to look at an income rider to provide options for the client if the market does correct and they wish to take income from another source besides their systematic withdrawal from equities and bonds.

I think if you were to talk to your prospective clients about these ideas, they would find more benefit to working with you. You might even speed up the sales process. More importantly, you provide a valuable benefit for those clients.

Winning Strategy: Dig deep into your client base. Ask more questions about assets held outside of your firm. Provide solutions that defer taxes and put your clients and their beneficiaries first.

How Guaranteed Income Drastically Changes Retirement Distribution

March 15, 2018

As I'm writing this (January 2018), it's hard to think about safety in a portfolio. The equity markets continue to rage with double-digit growth, as they have for the past several years. There seems to be a new stock market high just about every week, if not every day.

But accumulation and income are two different animals. They require two unique approaches to solve the client's problem.

Accumulation

Take a look at systematic contributions to a qualified plan like a 401(k) plan or a nonqualified systematic investment plan. As you make ongoing contributions, you buy more shares of the investment when the market (or specifically, the investment) is down. As the value of the investment increases, you purchase more shares and gain exponential value. The math phenomenon is called dollar cost averaging (DCA). By being disciplined and consistent, your average cost per share is less than the average paid per share due to your ability to buy more when the investment is down.

Distribution

If you are relying on systematic withdrawals during retirement, the opposite math phenomenon works against you. As you withdraw funds for income, you liquidate more shares when the market corrects. Therefore, you lose more shares when the market recovers. It multiplies your losses in a way. After the correction and recovery, you will have fewer units or shares than you would have with a steady market.

Guaranteed Income

Guaranteed income options provide stability in retirement income planning. Having a protected baseline of income reduces the pressure the portfolio might otherwise take on during the distribution phase. With guaranteed income, there is no need to reduce your unit holdings in order to generate the same level of income; thus, you have a better chance of protecting your assets for the long haul. The less you have to take out in a down market keeps more of the shares, or units, in assets under management for growth, inflation protection and capital gains treatment. There is nothing worse than paying tax on a liquidation that has corrected but still has embedded gains.

Take a look at using a guaranteed income tool to provide a floor for distribution planning. Your client benefits not only from the peace of mind, but also the ability to make their assets last longer during retirement.

Winning Strategy: Give guaranteed income options a look. By shifting the downside distribution risk to a guaranteed stream of income, the client can likely maintain their asset base longer in retirement.

4 Reasons You Should Focus on Retirement Income Planning

March 22, 2018

Over the next several decades, retirement income planning will only grow. Planners have so much opportunity to concentrate on income planning as a core competency. I spend a lot of time talking about Americans' behavior over the last 20 years and why income planning will be paramount for the next 20. Here are four reasons:

1. **Our savings rate continues to decline.** In December 2017, our savings rate dropped to 2.4 percent.[1] If you look at the past 20-year trend, you will see a steady decline in savings, with the exception of high inflation periods or around the dot-com bubble and financial crisis. This has left most people ill-equipped for retirement. Therefore, we will be asked to create more income from fewer assets than ever before in our careers. We have to get our clients to think differently, and the planning community will have to act differently to accomplish this.

2. **We continue to misuse social programs.** As I travel around the country, I always talk to clients who want to get their hands on their Social Security as soon as possible. They fear that the program will be bankrupt in the 2030s. There are some fixes to Social Security that will likely be addressed in future Congresses. For now, the bigger problem is the fact that we completely misuse the system. More than 50 percent of Americans take Social Security retirement early.[2] That makes your benefit smaller, and you lose the valuable 8 percent growth of your income between full retirement age and age 70. For some people, that equates to a 76 percent reduction in income. Only 2 percent of men and 4 percent of women take Social Security at age 70, so there is a lot of education that needs to happen in order to secure more guaranteed income.[2] With just a 20-year time frame, the difference could be as much as $122,000 in additional income. That makes a big difference for the typical retiree.

3. **Employers remain focused on shifting defined benefit plans to defined contribution plans.** That's good for many employees – low cost investing, multiple subaccounts to choose, tax deferral and matching employer contributions. But, the loss of guaranteed income creates a gap that needs to be filled. When I sit in a plan sponsor's office, I see a litany of risk-tolerance tests, return sheets and asset allocation brochures. But, when I ask the sponsor to tell me how their participants are going to turn these assets into income, their faces turn blank. Turning assets into dependable income is a priority and makes a baseline for many Americans to be able to buy the things they are accustomed to buying.

4. **In many minds, longevity grows as the most troubling risk for retirees.** The uncertainty around how long you will need income remains a fear for many Americans. Providing a plan to address this allows the client piece of mind and, if done properly, enhances the systematic withdrawal strategy. We are living longer often at the expense of our quality of life. Clients

need a plan to make sure they have not only lifetime income, but also a plan for when a long-term care emergency happens. The odds continue to increase that we will have a care event as we age. Shifting longevity risks for lifetime income and long-term care make sense in many cases. And, the shift of those risks is generally done for pennies on the dollar.

Income planning is a great spot to be in as a financial planner. There will be large numbers of people retiring and in need of income planning for many decades to come. Our past behaviors provide a reason to change our clients' perspectives and create value for them. I look forward to the challenge and the growth opportunities in this space.

Winning Strategy: Income is the ultimate outcome for many retirees. You can't spend assets, but you can spend income. Add retirement income planning to your discussions, and you'll add value to the client experience.

¹*Bureau of Economic Analysis, "Personal Income and Outlays, December 2017":* *https://www.bea.gov/newsreleases/national/pi/pinewsrelease.htm*
²*The Motley Fool, "When Does the Average American Start Collecting Social Security?" April 19, 2016: https://www.fool.com/retirement/general/2016/04/19/when-does-the-average-american-start-collecting-so.aspx*

Tax Control and Longevity Risk: Retirement Strategies Worth a Conversation

March 29, 2018

As I have talked with clients and advisors over the last six weeks, there is renewed optimism revolving around our economy. I share the same view and have shared it for some time. In January, I listened to the chief economist of an insurance carrier that had been lobbying for tax cuts for several years. It seems like the additional cash flow to corporations helps everyone's view and, possibly, company financials.

Risks of the Unknown

Tax control is really important in retirement planning. So much of our clients' savings is tied to qualified plans, either in company-provided retirement plans or individually owned IRAs. Many of these IRAs are funded with former employer-owned retirement plans as well. So, the tax status of these funds makes it difficult to plan for tax control at retirement. Generally, Roth options were not available in qualified plans until recently, so the majority of assets in these plans become fully taxable.

That's why proper use of nonqualified assets can come into play. It's important to consider taxes when making a plan. Even more important is the fact that longevity puts additional pressure on the taxation of the income as we age. Many income riders provide guaranteed income, but the income becomes fully taxable when the account value reaches zero. As longevity risks increase, nonqualified income can offset the impact of taxes later in life.

Once we hit life expectancy, the need for medical coverage and long-term care increases. With means-tested medical premiums, it will become critical to make sure we provide clients the lowest possible premium for their health care. The use of nonqualified income can reduce the tax burden on income and lower the means-tested income levels.

Take Control

You can control taxes and address longevity in multiple ways. Look for innovative planning techniques and tools to help the client protect their income while taking advantage of tax benefits and thresholds to maximize net income. Below are some ideas you should consider when evaluating tax control and opportunities with your clients:

- Look to convert traditional IRAs to Roth IRAs in the lower tax rate environment. This current tax payment allows the client to access funds tax free later with more distribution control (no required distributions at age 70½). The tax-free access can help keep them under a certain threshold for means-tested premiums or benefits.
- Consider using Home Equity Conversion Mortgages (HECMs) to shift some longevity risks. HECM lines of credit

give clients tax-free access to large sums of capital based on the value of their home. New rules allow the client to stay in their home through nonrecourse loans, irrespective of the future value of the home.

- Use nonqualified, single-premium annuities to maximize Social Security income payments by pushing the election date to age 70. Over 20 years, this can increase Social Security income by $122,000.
- Hedge longevity risks with nonqualified deferred income annuities. The exclusion ratio of DIAs can provide tax relief while supplying income later in life.

There are many more ways to control taxes while addressing longevity. Take a look at how guaranteed income and HECM options allow you to have more meaningful conversations with your clients. With more options, clients can rest easier knowing you have their best interests in mind.

Winning Strategy: You have to consider the tax effects now (and in the future) of the decisions that your clients make for retirement. Down the line, tax control becomes important as you rely more on rider income. And, as means testing becomes more prevalent, tax thresholds will be a critical success factor in any retirement plan.

Cost in Absence of Value

April 5, 2018

Throughout my sales career, several mentors have told me the catch phrase, "Cost is only an issue in the absence of value." Of course, I usually hear that and think about it from my perspective.

It's always important to add value to your business and personal relationships. But, when you talk about the added benefits of guaranteed income, you have to offset the cost with value. In many cases, the value of guaranteed income far outpaces the cost associated with the purchase of the vehicle to provide the guarantee.

Now, it's important to convey the same message to clients and not just sales teams. Specifically, we need to talk to company CEOs and human resource directors about the risk of their pension plans.

Cost of Pension Plans

Today, billions of dollars sit in defined pension plans that have been frozen by employers. Those pension plans are no longer helping to recruit new talent or retain existing employees. More worrisome are the expected increases to costs:

- The cost of administering a fully funded pension plan is guaranteed to increase by 25 percent by the end of 2019 due to the cost of Pension Benefit Guaranty Corporation (PBCG) premiums*
- For plans that are not fully funded, the cost of maintenance might increase as much as 33 percent by the end of 2019*

Those are real increases and real dollars that will be spent on an employee benefit that is not being leveraged to the full extent. So, the question is: Why would a company have a benefit that will increase in cost but doesn't provide any benefit?

I doubt any CEO would invest in a new plant or machinery that didn't provide suitable return. Especially with human capital, companies are reluctant to invest additional funds without a plan to grow production through that investment. They shouldn't do the same thing for an expensive employee benefit that doesn't provide value.

The cost of additional contributions is expensive. Life expectancies have increased, and returns are much lower than many old plan assumptions. Both of those result in funding shortages for a lot of defined benefit plans. Currently, CEOs are faced with making large contributions to bring the plan up to proper funding status. Since many are not willing to do that, they are left with the same problem year in and year out: an underfunded pension plan with no benefit to the organization. Well, it's about to create more of drain due to the cost increases from the PBGC premiums.

Value of Transfers

Myths exist around the pension risk transfer business. Many believe that a company has to write a huge check to cover their shortage. But in many cases, it makes sense to stagger the plan termination over a period of several years. Cash flow and capital requirements might make it easier to have a five to 10-year strategy instead of a one-time contribution.

Another myth is that lump-sum distributions don't help. In reality, lump-sum distributions can make a difference in the amount of shortage. Having educational meetings with employees can help the engagement level of lump-sum distributions. That's where a good income specialist can benefit the employee base. Retirement remains the most complicated problem most Americans will face; our industry needs to be face-to-face with as many people as possible.

Winning Strategy: Take the cost of the least valuable employee benefit off the table for companies. In doing so, you can help a greater number of people retire more securely.

*Pension Benefit Guaranty Corporation, Premium Rates, March 2018: https://www. pbgc.gov/prac/prem/premium-rates

How You Can Find More Clients with Pension Risk Transfer

April 12, 2018

Our sales team talks with a lot of advisors during our travels. Most conversations center around the need to grow the advisor's business.

As I've discussed before, part of The Go-Giver philosophy is the Law of Compensation: Your income is determined by how many people you serve and how well you serve them. Deploying this law through pension risk transfer sales can help drive your firm's revenue and increase the number of people you serve.

Pension risk transfers will be a significant market over the next decade. For advisors, it's a great way to meet prospective clients through a business contact. It opens the door to a group of employees with the approval of the human resource department or company leadership. What a great introduction to new people!

Companies of all sizes have pension liabilities that could hurt the enterprise. Pension plans carry longevity risk for the plan sponsors, interest rate risk for the pension fund managers and investment committee, and cost increases that concern C-suite leaders. When working on pension risk transfers, you can reduce or eliminate several problems for the employer:

1. Reduce a liability that shows up on the balance sheet (if not fully funded)

2. Avoid the increasing cost of administering the pension plan in the future

3. Shift the risk of employees living longer than funds can support payments

4. Eliminate the risk of interest rate fluctuations and equity market volatility

There are several reasons an employer would want a retirement income specialist in their office to talk with their employees about options on pension risk transfer decisions:

1. Lump-sum distributions to employees can reduce the funding gap in many plans

2. Employees are not well versed in their frozen pension plan and will benefit from expert guidance

3. Employees might have better options with individual rollovers of pension assets to better fit their personal and family wealth transfer goals

4. Individual IRAs typically have more options for beneficiary designations

Pension risk transfers create a win-win-win scenario for the advisor, the employer and the employees. The employees gain the advantage of talking to a retirement expert on-site, which is viewed as an added benefit at no cost to the employer. The employer gains the ability to transfer their risk to an insurance carrier, and eliminate or reduce the risks to their balance sheet and cost structure of maintaining a pension plan. The advisor wins by helping more people and serving them more effectively, which is the basis of the Law of Compensation.

Winning Strategy: Grow your clientele and help more people with their most complex problem – retirement. You can do both by working in the pension risk transfer market.

Missing the Shot You Didn't Take

April 19, 2018

I can never resist talking basketball in the spring, especially around the NCAA tournament and the final stretches of the NBA season.

For anyone who knows me, my recreational basketball skill set is focused on offense, not defense. Specifically, my game is played between the two 3-point lines. I usually don't leave a game thinking I should have taken a shot but didn't. A lot of coaches tell players that they will never make the shot they don't take.

Recently, one of my best wholesalers posed a question to the rest of our sales team. He asked how often clients wish they had bought something a year ago but didn't have the faith to make the decision.

Think about how many people wish they had bought stock a few years ago. Then, think about how many wish they had sold it while it was at an all-time high. That's always the case – clients always wish they had done something a year ago.

So here's my question: What will you wish you had done this year when you look back at your business next year?

One Possible Answer

Pension risk transfer is an opportunity to drive revenue in your practice for 2018 and beyond. However, many are reluctant to pursue this market because it has a long gestation period before you receive revenue or commission. I think there are several reasons to evolve your financial planning practice to include pension risk transfers:

1. Current tax law allows companies to make deductible contributions to their 2017 pension shortage at the higher tax rate of 35 percent. This equates to a 14 percent discount for applying contributions to the pension shortage in 2018.

2. With our recent strategic partnership, Ash Brokerage can provide fee income to financial advisors before product is placed and while the company completes the termination process.

3. More and more large companies are taking advantage of shifting pension risk to insurance companies. Small and midsized companies tend to follow larger corporations, and most pension assets rest with small businesses.

4. Bond yields will likely change dramatically over the next 36 months, putting pressure on the fixed income portion of the investment portfolio. The same can be said for the recent volatility in the equity markets. It makes it difficult for plan sponsors to manage the risk for investment yields.

5. Life expectancies continue to increase for older workers. That puts more obligation on the plan assets to provide lifetime income to the plan participants. That translates into more risk for the plan sponsor.

Current economic and tax climates make now a great time to talk about pension risk transfers. If you don't begin integrating it into your practice today, you will likely look back a year from now and say that you wished that you had done so. Don't wish you had done something a year ago that is now costing you business. Take a good look at pension risk transfers as a larger part of your business.

Winning Strategy: Don't look back a year from now and wish you had added pension risk transfers to your business. The climate is ripe to take advantage of a business opportunity that might not come by again.

Shift the Risk, Not the Return

April 26, 2018

Lately, I've spent a lot of time talking about pension risk transfers. I think it's a market that will explode over the next 12-18 months for any financial professional who is committed to talking with CEOs and human resources leaders.

But, saving on premiums and taking a less valuable employee benefit off the table is only part of the benefit. The real benefit is the shifting of risk. Plan sponsors bear several risks that can be reduced or eliminated.

The Real Risks

Pension plan sponsors take on the investment risk of plan assets. Regardless of economic projections, managing risk will likely be more difficult within a plan for the immediate future. Rising interest rates will result in lower bond valuations. A choppy market will make it difficult to have steady returns necessary to hit funding targets.

Life expectancies continue to increase in the United States. There is a requirement to pay the monthly income stated in the pension plan document. Regardless of how long the plan participant lives, the plan must meet that obligation. The problem is that the current funding status for many plans is below 100 percent, so the plan might not have enough assets to meet those obligations.

The same problems exist for most retirees. They ask, "Do I have enough assets to generate the income I need? Will I live too long and exhaust those assets?" Unfortunately, business owners and leaders must answer those questions for themselves, as well as for all their employees. The fact that business owners have an added responsibility for their employees' retirement creates more stress and anxiety.

Worth the Shift

These risks can be shifted through pension risk transfer. The process is long, but it can be easy, seamless and cost-effective for business owners. There is little reason to keep risk on your balance sheet when there are alternatives. Unfortunately, most business owners don't know about the options available to them. It makes a great conversation for you to have with business owners: Shift this risk, and you will gain the trust of the entire company.

Winning Strategy: Shift the longevity risks for corporations in a similar fashion to individual retirement plans. Take away investment risks and the potential of living too long, and you'll gain a corporate client plus all the employees.

Afterword

ABC: Always Be Changing

The past two years in the financial services industry have been the most tumultuous I can remember in my 25-plus-year career. It started with the introduction of the U.S. Department of Labor's Fiduciary Standard and Conflict of Interest Rule in April 2016. Much of this book pertains to the transition to the rule – it's been quite the roller-coaster ride over the last two years.

In March of 2018, the future of our industry got cloudier with a decision in the U.S. District Court that ruled against the DOL's standards. Regardless of where we stand from a regulatory environment – now or in the future – our industry continues to change. And, it should always look to evolve to better serve our clients.

The regulatory environment should not dictate what our clients are demanding. Today, clients want more transparency in their products and services. They want to know that we are working in their best interests and be assured that we remain committed to their needs first. That should be a table stake for a client relationship. We need to get to a point where clients can hold us to the same level of trust as their other professional relationships – their doctor, attorney, CPA, banker, etc. That shift has begun, but it needs to accelerate.

I feel we need to concentrate our efforts on a few key elements to continue the shift:

1. Focus on the client experience. In today's financial system, we can apply for mortgages and deposit checks via our phones. Why can't we purchase a retirement income strategy the same way, with the same speed and the same accuracy? Our carriers need to reinvest in our collective businesses to ensure that we stay up to speed on technology. Ultimately, we have to make it easier to do business so our clients will leverage our advice and purchase our solutions.

2. Eliminate our biases. Many firms believe they can only work in their client's best interest if they charge a fee based on assets under management. I disagree. Looking at the industry and the need for guaranteed income and protection solutions, the assets under management pricing strategy includes as many conflicts of interest as commissions. The product pricing should largely be irrelevant – assuming the platform consists of only quality firms with appropriate product pricing that meets the needs of our clients. We have to reduce the focus on our business model and reflect on our clients' goals and objectives.

3. Concentrate on education. Clients view financial services and products as the most complex of all the things they purchase. Because of that perception, they generally do not want to take the time to learn about how guaranteed income benefits their retirement portfolios. In order to make that change, we have to be better educators. In fact, I suggest that providing education is the best value proposition we can deliver. The more value we can provide, the better chance we have at capturing clients and solving their needs.

There are multiple issues that our industry faces in the coming years. Regulation should not shape our industry; instead, we should define how our industry delivers products and services to our clients. It's unfortunate that the general public doesn't like how we are performing and must rely on regulators to define who we are.

I challenge everyone to take a hard look at their business. Think how to best serve your clients and how to serve more of them, and your revenue will grow. If you drive value through your client base – and value that is important to them – it is inevitable that they will take your lead to secure their financial future.

Be less of a commodity by being more of you and less of a software package or product. In a movie, Alec Baldwin once told us ABC stood for "always be closing." That doesn't apply anymore. In order to succeed, grow, evolve and transform, I think ABC means "always be changing." My hope is that you become an agent of change for this industry with the ideas and strategies from this book.

Good Selling,

26624909R00117

Made in the USA
Columbia, SC
18 September 2018